PROGRAM OF THE COMMUNIST PARTY
OF THE SOVIET UNION

PROGRAM of the COMMUNIST PARTY of the SOVIET UNION

*With a Special Preface
to the American Edition
by N. S. KHRUSHCHEV*

INTERNATIONAL PUBLISHERS
NEW YORK

Library of Congress Catalog Card Number: 63–23083

Manufactured in the United States of America

Special Preface to the American Edition

It gives me great pleasure to write a brief preface to the United States edition of so important a document as the Program of the Communist Party of the Soviet Union.

Possibly some people will wonder if there is any sense in Americans acquainting themselves with the program of a political party functioning in another country far beyond the borders of the United States.

In my opinion this will be of some value.

In the modern world an understanding of the goals and aspirations of other peoples takes on tremendous significance, especially in the case of the people of the Soviet Union or of the United States, both of whom are exerting such a great influence on the destiny of mankind.

The Communist Party of the Soviet Union is the guiding force in Soviet society and in the government of the USSR. Its program is, of course, a party program. But it has been discussed and approved by the entire Soviet people as well; it must therefore be considered an expression of the national goals of the Soviet Union and its plans for the future.

I am confident that even those far removed from Marxist philosophy will easily understand the ideas, the aims, the basic content of this program. It is a program of creation—creation in industry and agriculture, in science and culture, in the field of human relations and morality.

An indispensable condition for creation is peace. This is especially true today when man possesses a means of destruction and extermination monstrous in its power. Those persons who read our program without prejudice no doubt will recognize that statements by Communists of the Soviet Union about peace are not empty declarations, not propaganda, but the expression of their deepest and most vital interests.

We are firmly convinced of the victory of communism and we have a plan with the aid of which we expect to attain communism. This plan is set forth quite fully in the Program of the CPSU. In reading it, I hope, you yourself will become convinced that it is not a plan of secret conspiracies or military threats but a plan for peaceful competition between the two systems.

We are firmly of the opinion that in the course of peaceful competition the peoples will be able to satisfy themselves as to which social system secures them a higher standard of living, greater assurance for the future, freer access to education and culture, more perfect forms of democracy and personal freedom.

We have no doubt that in such competition communism will win. Certainly not all Americans will agree with my views. But anyone with common sense must surely agree that competition between the two systems under conditions of peace in no way constitutes a threat to any nation. On the contrary, all nations can only gain from it.

Communists have no other goal than the achievement of happiness by all the people on earth. In the Program of the CPSU it is stated:

"Communism accomplishes the historic mission of delivering all men from social inequality, from every form of oppression and exploitation, from the horrors of war, and proclaims *Peace, Labor, Freedom, Equality, Fraternity, and Happiness* for all peoples of the earth."

Becoming acquainted with the program of communist construction in the Soviet Union will help Americans better to understand the essence of the Soviet system, the aspirations and true goals of the Soviet people. And this, in my profound conviction, will further the growth of friendship between our great peoples and therefore strengthen peace throughout the world as well.

N. S. KHRUSHCHEV

6

Contents

THE TRANSITION FROM CAPITALISM TO COMMUNISM IS THE ROAD OF HUMAN PROGRESS

THE TASKS OF THE COMMUNIST PARTY OF THE SOVIET UNION IN BUILDING A COMMUNIST SOCIETY

7

PROGRAM OF THE COMMUNIST PARTY
OF THE SOVIET UNION

Introduction

The Great October Socialist Revolution ushered in a new era in the history of mankind, the era of the downfall of capitalism and the establishment of communism. Socialism has triumphed in the Soviet Union and has achieved decisive victories in the People's Democracies; socialism has become the practical cause of hundreds of millions of people, and the banner of the revolutionary movement of the working class throughout the world.

More than a hundred years ago Karl Marx and Frederick Engels, the great teachers of the proletariat, wrote in the Communist Manifesto: "*A specter is haunting Europe, the specter of communism.*" The courageous and selfless struggle of the proletarians of all countries brought mankind nearer to communism. First dozens and hundreds of people, and then thousands and millions, inspired by the ideals of communism, stormed the old world. The Paris Commune, the October Revolution, the socialist revolutions in China and in a number of European and Asian countries are the major historical stages in the heroic battles fought by the international working class for the victory of communism. A tremendously long road, a road drenched in the blood of fighters for the happiness of the people, a road of glorious victories and temporary reverses, had to be traversed before *communism, which was once no more than a dream, became the greatest force of modern times, a society that is being built up over vast areas of the globe.*

In the early twentieth century the center of the international revolutionary movement shifted to Russia. Russia's heroic working class, led by the Bolshevik Party headed by Vladimir Ilyich Lenin, became its vanguard. The Communist Party inspired and led the socialist revolution; it was the organizer and leader of the first workers' and peasants' state in history. The brilliant genius of Lenin, the great teacher of the working people of the world, whose name will live forever, illuminates mankind's road to communism.

On entering the arena of political struggle, the Leninist Communist Party raised high the banner of revolutionary Marxism over the world. Marxism-Leninism became a powerful ideological weapon for the revolutionary transformation of society. At every historical stage the Party, taking guidance from the theory of Marx, Engels, and Lenin, accomplished the tasks scientifically formulated in its programs.

In adopting its *first Program* at its Second Congress in 1903, the Bolshevik Party called on the working class and all working people of Russia to fight for the overthrow of the tsarist autocracy and then of the bourgeois system and for the establishment of the dictatorship of the proletariat. In February 1917 the tsarist regime was swept away. In October 1917 the proletarian revolution abolished the capitalist system so hated by the people. *A socialist country came into being for the first time in history. The creation of a new world began.*

The first Program of the Party had been carried out.

Adopting its *second Program* at its Eighth Congress in 1919, the Party promulgated the task of building a socialist society. Treading on unexplored ground and overcoming difficulties and hardships, the Soviet people under the leadership of the Communist Party put into practice the plan for socialist construction drawn up by Lenin. *Socialism triumphed in the Soviet Union completely and finally.*

The second Program of the Party had likewise been carried out.

The gigantic revolutionary exploit accomplished by the Soviet people has roused and inspired the masses in all countries and continents. A mighty purifying thunderstorm marking the springtime of mankind is raging over the earth. *The socialist revolutions in European and Asian countries have resulted in the establishment of the world socialist system.* A powerful wave of national liberation revolutions is sweeping away the colonial system of imperialism.

One-third of mankind is building a new life under the banner of scientific communism. The first contingents of the working class to shake off capitalist oppression are facilitating victory for fresh contingents of their class brothers. The socialist world is expanding; the capitalist world is shrinking. Socialism will inevitably succeed capitalism everywhere. Such is the objective law of social development. Imperialism is powerless to check the irresistible process of emancipation.

Our epoch, whose main content is the transition from capitalism to socialism, is an epoch of struggle between the two opposing social systems, an epoch of socialist and national liberation revolutions, of the breakdown of imperialism and the abolition of the colonial system, an epoch of the transition of more and more peoples to the socialist path, of the triumph of socialism and communism on a world wide scale. The central factor of the present epoch is the international working class and its main creation, the world socialist system.

Today the Communist Party of the Soviet Union (CPSU) is adopting its third Program, a program for the building of communist society. The new Program is a constructive generalization of the experience of socialist development, it takes account of the experience of the revolutionary movement throughout the world and, giving expression to the collective opinion of the Party, defines the main tasks and principal stages of communist construction.

The supreme goal of the Party is to build a communist society on whose banner will be inscribed: "From each according to his ability, to each according to his needs." The Party's motto, "Everything for the sake of man, for the benefit of man," will be put into effect in full.

The Communist Party of the Soviet Union, true to proletarian internationalism, always follows the militant slogan "Workers of all countries, unite!" *The Party regards communist construction in the USSR as the Soviet people's great internationalist task,* in keeping with the interests of the world socialist system as a whole and with the interests of the international proletariat and all mankind.

Communism accomplishes the historic mission of delivering all men from social inequality, from every form of oppression and exploitation, from the horrors of war, and proclaims *Peace, Labor, Freedom, Equality, Fraternity, and Happiness* for all peoples of the earth.

Part One

THE TRANSITION FROM CAPITALISM TO COMMUNISM IS THE ROAD OF HUMAN PROGRESS

I. The Historical Necessity of the Transition from Capitalism to Socialism

The epoch-making turn of mankind from capitalism to socialism, initiated by the October Revolution, is a natural result of the development of society. Marxism-Leninism discovered the objective laws of social development and revealed the contradictions inherent in capitalism, the inevitability of their bringing about a revolutionary explosion, and of the transition of society to communism.

Capitalism is the last exploiting system. Having developed its productive forces to an enormous extent, it became a tremendous obstacle to social progress. Capitalism alone is responsible for the fact that the twentieth century, a century of colossal growth of the productive forces and of great scientific progress, has not yet put an end to the poverty of hundreds of millions of people, has not provided an abundance of material and spiritual values for all men on earth. The growing conflict between productive forces and production relations imperatively demands that mankind should break the decayed capitalist shell, release the powerful productive forces created by man and use them for the good of society as a whole.

Whatever the specific character of the rise and development of capitalism in any country, that system has everywhere common features and objective laws.

The development of world capitalism and of the revolutionary struggle of the working class has fully confirmed the correctness of the Marxist-Leninist analysis of capitalism and its highest stage, imperialism, given in the first and second Programs of the Party. The basic propositions of this analysis are also given below in the present Program.

Under capitalism, the basic and decisive means of production belong to the numerically small class of capitalists and landowners, while the vast majority of the population consists of proletarians and semi-proletarians, who own no means of production and are therefore compelled to sell their labor power and by their labor create profits and riches for the ruling classes of society. The bourgeois state, whatever its form, is an instrument of the domination of labor by capital.

The development of large-scale capitalist production—production for profit, for the appropriation of surplus value—leads to the elimination of small independent producers, makes them wholly dependent on capital. Capitalism extensively exploits female and child labor. The economic laws of its development necessarily give rise to a huge army of unemployed, which is constantly replenished by ruined peasants and urban petty bourgeoisie. The exploitation of the working class and all working people is continuously increasing, social inequality is becoming more and more marked, the gulf between the haves and have-nots is widening, and the sufferings and privations of the millions are growing worse.

Capitalism, by concentrating millions of workers in its factories, socializing the process of labor, imparts a social character to production; nevertheless it is the capitalists who appropriate the fruits of labor. This fundamental contradiction of capitalism—the contradiction between the social character of production and the private capitalist form of appropriation—manifests itself in production anarchy and in the fact that the purchasing power of society falls short of the expansion of production and leads periodically to destructive economic crises. Crises and periods of industrial stagnation, in turn, are still more ruinous to small producers, increase the dependence of wage labor on capital and lead more rapidly to a relative, and sometimes an absolute, deterioration of the condition of the working class.

The growth and development of the contradictions of bourgeois society are accompanied by the growing discontent of the working people and the exploited masses with the capitalist system, by an increase in the number of proletarians and their greater unity, and by a sharpening of their struggle against the exploiters. At the same time there is an accelerated *creation of the material conditions that make possible the replacement of capitalist by communist production relations, that is, the accom-*

plishment of the social revolution which is the aim of the Communist Party, the politically conscious exponent of the class movement of the proletariat.

The working class, which is the most consistent revolutionary class, is the chief motive force of the revolutionary transformation of the world. In the course of class struggles it becomes organized, sets up its trade unions and political parties, and wages an economic, political, and theoretical struggle against capitalism. In fulfilling its historic mission as the revolutionary remaker of the old society and creator of a new system, the working class becomes the exponent, not only of its own class interests, but of the interests of all working people. It is the natural leader of all forces fighting against capitalism.

The dictatorship of the proletariat and the leadership of the Marxist-Leninist party are indispensable conditions for the triumph of the socialist revolution and the building of socialism. The firm alliance of the working class and the working peasant masses under the leadership of the working class is the supreme principle of the dictatorship of the proletariat.

The process of concentration and centralization of capital, while destroying free competition, led in the early twentieth century to the establishment of powerful capitalist monopoly associations—syndicates, cartels, and trusts—which acquired decisive importance in the economy, led to the merging of bank capital and immensely concentrated industrial capital, and to intensive export of capital. The trusts, which encompassed entire groups of capitalist powers, began the economic division of a world already divided territorially among the wealthiest countries. Capitalism had entered its final stage, the stage of monopoly capitalism, of imperialism.

The period of a more or less smooth spread of capitalism all over the globe gave way to spasmodic, cataclysmic development causing an unprecedented growth and aggravation of all the contradictions of capitalism—economic, political, class, and national. The imperialist powers' struggle for markets, for spheres of capital investment, for raw materials and labor, and for world domination became more intense than ever. In an epoch of the undivided rule of imperialism, that struggle necessarily led to devastating wars.

Imperialism is decaying and moribund capitalism: it is the eve of the socialist revolution. *The world capitalist system as a whole is ripe for the social revolution of the proletariat.*

The exceedingly high degree of development of world capitalism in general; the replacement of free competition by state monopoly capitalism; the establishment by banks, as well as by associations of capitalists, of machinery for the social regulation of production and the distribution of products; the growing cost of living and the oppression of the working class by the trusts connected with the growth of capitalist monopolies; the enslavement of the working class by the imperialist state, and the immensely increased difficulty of the economic and political struggle of the proletariat; and the horrors, hardships, and ruination brought about by imperialist war—have all made inevitable the downfall of capitalism and the transition to a higher type of social economy.

The revolutionary break-up of imperialism does not take place all over the world simultaneously. The uneven character of the economic and political development of the capitalist countries under imperialism leads to revolutions occurring at different periods in different countries. V. I. Lenin developed the theory of the socialist revolution in new historical conditions, elaborated the theory of the possibility of socialism triumphing first in one capitalist country taken singly.

Russia was the weakest link in the imperialist system and the focal point of all its contradictions. On the other hand, all the conditions necessary for the victory of socialism arose there. Her working class was the most revolutionary and best organized in the world and had considerable experience of class struggle. It was led by a Marxist-Leninist party armed with an advanced revolutionary theory and steeled in class battles.

The Bolshevik Party brought together in one revolutionary torrent the struggle of the working class for socialism, the country-wide peace movement, the peasants' struggle for land, and the national liberation movement of the oppressed peoples of Russia, and directed these forces to the overthrow of capitalism.

II. The Historic Significance of the October Revolution and of the Victory of Socialism in the USSR

The Great October Revolution breached the imperialist front in Russia, one of the world's largest countries, firmly established the dictatorship of the proletariat and created a new type of state, the Soviet socialist state, and a new type of democracy, democracy for the working people.

Workers' and peasants' power, born of the revolution, took Russia out of the bloodbath of the imperialist war, saved her from the national catastrophe to which the exploiting classes had doomed her, and delivered her peoples from the danger of enslavement by foreign capital.

The October Revolution undermined the economic basis of a system of exploitation and social injustice. Soviet power nationalized industry, the railways, banks, and the land. It abolished the landlord system and fulfilled the peasants' age-long dream of land.

The October Revolution smashed the chains of national oppression; it proclaimed and put into effect the right of nations to self-determination, up to and including the right to secede. The Revolution completely abolished the social-estate and class privileges of the exploiters. For the first time in history, it emancipated women and granted them the same rights as men.

The socialist revolution in Russia shook the entire structure of world capitalism to its very foundations; the world split into two opposing systems.

For the first time there emerged in the international arena a state which put forward the great slogan of peace and began carrying through new principles in relations between peoples and countries. Mankind acquired a reliable bulwark in its struggle against wars of conquest, for peace and the security of the peoples.

The October Revolution led the country on to the road of socialism. The path which the Soviet people were to traverse was an unexplored and arduous one. The reactionary forces of the old world did all they could to strangle the Soviet state at

its birth. The young Soviet Republic had to cope with intervention and civil war, economic blockade and disruption, conspiracies, sabotage, subversion, terrorism, and numerous other trials.
Socialist construction was rendered incredibly difficult by the
socio-economic, technical and cultural backwardness of the country. The victorious workers and peasants lacked knowledge of
state administration and the experience necessary for the construction of a new society. The difficulties of socialist construction were greatly increased by the fact that for almost thirty
years the USSR was the world's only socialist state, and was
subjected to sharp attacks by the hostile capitalist encirclement.
The class struggle in the period of transition from capitalism to
socialism was therefore acute.

The enemies of Leninism maintained that Russia was not mature enough for a socialist revolution, that it was impossible to
build socialism in one country. But the enemies of Leninism
were put to shame.

A wise, discerning policy, the greatest staunchness, organization,
and deep faith in their own strength and in the strength of the
people were required of the Party of the working class. It was
necessary to steer the right course in socialist construction and
ensure the victory of socialism, despite the highly complicated
international situation and a relatively weak industrial base, in
a country whose economy had been badly ravaged by war and
where small-commodity production was overwhelmingly predom-
inant.

The Party proved equal to that historic task. Under the leadership of Lenin it worked out a plan for the radical transformation
of the country, for the construction of socialism. On the basis
of a thorough scientific analysis, Lenin elaborated the policy
of the proletarian state for the entire period of transition from
capitalism to socialism. He evolved the New Economic Policy
(NEP), designed to bring about the victory of socialism. The
main elements of the Lenin plan for the building of a socialist
society were industrialization of the country, agricultural cooperation, and the cultural revolution.

The Party upheld that plan in an acute struggle against
sceptics and capitulators, against the Trotskyists, Right oppor-

tunists, nationalist deviators, and other hostile groups. It rallied the whole of the Soviet people to the struggle to put Lenin's program into practice.

The point at issue at the time was: either perish or forge full steam ahead and overtake the capitalist countries economically.

The Soviet state had first of all to solve the problem of *industrialization*. In a historically brief period, without outside help, the Soviet Union built up a large-scale modern industry. By the time it had fulfilled three five-year plans (1929-41) the Soviet Union had become a mighty industrial power that had achieved complete economic independence from the capitalist countries. Its defense capacity had increased immeasurably. *The industrialization of the USSR was a great exploit performed by the working class and the people as a whole,* for they spared no effort or means, and consciously made sacrifices to lift the country out of its backward state.

The destiny of socialism in a country like the USSR largely depended on the solution of a most difficult problem, namely, the transition from a small-scale, dispersed peasant economy to *socialist cooperation.* Led by the Party, aided and fully supported by the working class, the peasantry took the road of socialism. Millions of small individual farms went into voluntary association to form collective farms. A large number of Soviet state farms and machine and tractor stations were established. The introduction in the Soviet countryside of large-scale socialist farming meant *a far-reaching revolution in economic relations, in the entire way of life of the peasantry.* Collectivization forever delivered the countryside from kulak bondage, from class differentiation, ruin, and poverty. The real solution of the eternal peasant question was provided by the Lenin cooperative plan.

To build socialism it was necessary to raise the cultural level of the people; this too was accomplished successfully. A *cultural revolution* was carried out in the country. It freed the working people from spiritual slavery and ignorance and gave them access to the cultural values accumulated by mankind. The country, the bulk of whose population had been illiterate, made breath-taking progress in science and culture.

Socialism, which Marx and Engels scientifically predicted as

*inevitable and the plan for the construction of which was mapped
out by Lenin, has become a reality in the Soviet Union.*

Socialism has done away forever with the supremacy of private
ownership of the means of production, that source of the division of society into antagonistic classes. Socialist ownership of
the means of production has become the solid economic foundation of society. Unlimited opportunities have been afforded for
the development of the productive forces.

Socialism has solved a great social problem—it has abolished
the exploiting classes and the causes engendering the exploitation of man by man. There are now two friendly classes in the
USSR—the working class and the peasantry. And these classes,
furthermore, have changed. The common character of the two
forms of socialist property has brought the working class and the
collective-farm peasantry close together; it has strengthened their
alliance and made their friendship indestructible. A new intelligentsia, coming from the people and devoted to socialism, has
emerged. The one-time antithesis between town and countryside, between labor by hand and by brain, has been abolished.
The indestructible socio-political and ideological unity of the
Soviet people has been built on the basis of the common vital
interests of the workers, peasants, and intellectuals.

The socialist principle "From each according to his abilities,
to each according to his work" has been put into effect in the
Soviet Union. This principle ensures that the members of society have a material interest in the fruits of their labor; it makes
it possible to harmonize personal and social interests in the most
effective way and serves as a powerful stimulus for increasing
productivity of labor, developing the economy and raising the
people's standard of living. The awareness that they work for
themselves and their society and not for exploiters inspires the
working people with labor enthusiasm; it encourages their effort
for innovation, their creative initiative, and mass socialist emulation. Socialism is creative effort by the working masses. The
growing activity of the people in the building of a new life is a
law of the socialist epoch.

The aim of socialism is to meet the growing material and

cultural requirements of the people ever more fully by continuously developing and improving social production.

The entire life of socialist society is based on the principle of broad *democracy*. Working people take an active part, through the Soviets, trade unions, and other mass organizations, in managing the affairs of the state and in solving problems of economic and cultural advancement. Socialist democracy includes both political freedoms—freedom of speech, of the press and of assembly, the right to elect and to be elected—and also social rights, the right to work, to rest and leisure, to free education and free medical services, to material security in old age and in case of illness or disability; equality of citizens of all races and nationalities; equal rights for women and men in all spheres of political, economic, and cutural activity. Socialist democracy, unlike bourgeois democracy, does not merely proclaim the rights of the people, but guarantees that they are really implemented. Soviet society ensures the real liberty of the individual. The highest manifestation of this liberty is man's emancipation from exploitation, which is what primarily constitutes genuine social justice.

Socialism has created the most favorable conditions for the rapid progress of science. The achievements of Soviet science clearly show the superiority of the socialist system and testify to the unlimited possibilities of scientific progress and to the growing role of science under socialism. It is only logical that the country of victorious socialism should have ushered in the era of the utilization of atomic energy for peaceful purposes, and that it should have blazed a trail into outer space. The man-made satellites of the earth and the sun, powerful space rockets and interplanetary spaceships, atomic power stations and the first triumphal orbitings of the globe, accomplished by Soviet citizens, which are a source of pride to all mankind, have become symbols of the creative energy of ascendant communism.

The solution of the *national question* is one of the greatest achievements of socialism. This question is of especial importance to a country like the Soviet Union, inhabited by more than a hundred nations and nationalities. Socialist society has not only guaranteed the political equality of nations and created Soviet national statehood, but has also abolished the economic and cultural inequality inherited from the old system. With reciprocal fraternal assistance, primarily from the great Russian people, all the Soviet non-Russian republics have set up their own modern industries, trained their own national working class and intelligentsia, and developed a culture that is national in form and socialist in content. Many peoples which in the past were backward have achieved socialism, by-passing the capitalist stage of development. The union and consolidation of equal peoples on a voluntary basis in a single multi-national state—the Union of Soviet Socialist Republics—their close cooperation in state, economic, and cultural development, their fraternal friendship and flourishing economy and culture constitute the most important result of Leninist national policy.

To the Soviet people fell the historic role of starting on a new road, of blazing a new path of social development. This required special efforts, a continuous quest for forms and methods of building the new society that had to be tested in the crucible of life. For nearly two out of little more than four decades, the Soviet people were compelled to devote their energies to the repulsion of invasions by the imperialist powers and to postwar economic rehabilitation. The Soviet system was put to a particularly severe test during the Great Patriotic War, the most trying war in history. By winning that war, the Soviet people proved that there are no forces in the world capable of stopping the progress of socialist society.

What are the principal lessons to be learned from the experience of the Soviet people?

Soviet experience has shown that the peoples are able to achieve socialism only as a result of *the socialist revolution and the establishment of the dictatorship of the proletariat.* Despite certain specific features due to the concrete historical conditions of socialist construction in the Soviet Union, then in a hostile capitalist encirclement, this experience has fully confirmed the fundamental principles of socialist revolution and socialist construction, principles which are of universal significance.

Soviet experience has shown that socialism alone can put an end to the exploitation of man by man, production anarchy, economic crises, unemployment, and the poverty of the people, and ensure planned, continuous and rapid development of the economy and steady improvement of the people's standard of living.

Soviet experience has shown that the working class can fulfil its historic mission as the builder of a new society only in a firm *alliance with the non-proletarian working masses,* primarily the peasantry.

Soviet experience has shown that the victory of the socialist revolution alone provides all possibilities and conditions for the abolition of all national oppression, *for the voluntary union of free and equal nations and nationalities in a single state.*

Soviet experience has shown that *the socialist state* is the main instrument for the socialist transformation of society. The state organizes and unites the masses, exercises planned leadership of economic and cultural construction, and safeguards the revolutionary gains of the people.

Soviet experience has shown that *socialism and peace are inseparable.* The might of socialism serves peace. The Soviet Union saved mankind from fascist enslavement. The Soviet state, which champions peace and implements the Leninist principle of the peaceful coexistence of states with different social systems, is a mighty barrier to imperialist aggression.

Soviet experience has fully borne out the Marxist-Leninist theory that *the Communist Party plays a decisive role* in the formation and development of socialist society. Only a party that steadfastly pursues a class, proletarian policy, and is equipped with progressive, revolutionary theory, only a party solidly united and closely linked with the masses, can organize the people and lead them to the victory of socialism.

Soviet experience has shown that fidelity *to the principles of Marxism-Leninism, of proletarian internationalism,* their firm and unswerving implementation and defense against all enemies and opportunists, are imperative conditions for the victory of socialism.

The world's greatest revolution and the socialist reorganization of society, which has attained unprecedented heights in its development and prosperity, have confirmed in practice *the his-*

torical truth of Leninism and have delivered a crushing blow to social-reformist ideology.

As a result of the devoted labor of the Soviet people and the theoretical and practical activities of the Communist Party of the Soviet Union, *there exists in the world a socialist society that is a reality and a science of socialist construction that has been tested in practice. The highroad to socialism has been paved.* Many peoples are already marching along it, and it will be taken sooner or later by all peoples.

III. The World Socialist System

The Soviet Union is pursuing the tasks of communist construction not alone but in fraternal community with the other socialist countries.

The defeat of German fascism and Japanese militarism in the Second World War, in which the Soviet Union played the decisive part, created favorable conditions for the overthrow of capitalist and landlord rule by the peoples in a number of European and Asian countries. The peoples of Albania, Bulgaria, China, Czechoslovakia, the Democratic Republic of Vietnam, the German Democratic Republic, Hungary, the Korean People's Democratic Republic, Poland, and Rumania, and still earlier the people of the Mongolian People's Republic, adopted the path of socialist construction and, together with the Soviet Union, have formed the socialist camp. Yugoslavia likewise took the socialist path. But the Yugoslav leaders by their revisionist policy contraposed Yugoslavia to the socialist camp and the international Communist movement, thus threatening the loss of the revolutionary gains of the Yugoslav people.

The socialist revolutions in Europe and Asia dealt imperialism a further powerful blow. The victory of the revolution in China was of special importance. The revolutions in European and Asian countries are the biggest event in world history since October 1917.

A new form of political organization of society, *people's democracy,* a variety of the dictatorship of the proletariat, emerged. It reflected the distinctive development of socialist revolution at a time when imperialism had been weakened and the balance of forces had tilted in favor of socialism. It also reflected the distinctive historical and national features of the various countries.

There emerged a world socialist system, a social, economic and political community of free sovereign peoples pursuing the socialist and communist path, united by an identity of interests and goals and the close bonds of international socialist solidarity.

In the People's Democracies socialist production relations are dominant and the socio-economic possibility of capitalist restoration has been eliminated. The successes of these countries have conclusively proved that true progress in all lands, irrespective of the level of their economic development, their area and population, is feasible only under socialism.

The combined forces of the socialist camp guarantee each socialist country against encroachments by imperialist reaction. The consolidation of the socialist countries in a single camp, its increasing unity and steadily growing strength, ensures the complete victory of socialism and communism within the framework of the system as a whole.

The countries of the socialist system have accumulated considerable collective experience in the remodeling of the lives of hundreds of millions of people and have contributed many new and specific features to the forms of political and economic organization of society. This experience is a most valuable asset to the international revolutionary movement.

It has been borne out in practice and recognized by all Marxist-Leninist parties that the processes of socialist revolution and construction are founded on a number of *basic objective laws* applicable to all countries entering upon the socialist path.

The world socialist system is *a new type of economic and political relationship between countries.* The socialist countries have the same type of economic basis, social ownership of means of production; the same type of political system, rule of the people with the working class at their head; a common ideology, Marxism-Leninism; common interests in the defense of their revolutionary gains and national independence from encroachments by the imperialist camp; and a great common goal, communism. This socio-economic and political community constitutes the objective groundwork for lasting and friendly inter-governmental relations within the socialist camp. The distinctive features of the relations existing between the countries of the socialist community are complete equality, mutual respect for independence and sovereignty, and fraternal mutual assistance and cooperation. In the socialist camp or, which is the same thing, in the world community of socialist countries, none have, nor can have, any special rights or privileges.

The experience of the world socialist system has confirmed the need for the *closest unity* of countries that fall away from capitalism, for their united effort in the building of socialism and communism. The line of socialist construction in isolation, detached from the world community of socialist countries, is theoretically untenable because it conflicts with the objective laws governing the development of socialist society. It is harmful economically because it causes waste of social labor, retards the rates of growth of production, and makes the country dependent upon the capitalist world. It is reactionary and dangerous politically because it does not unite, but divides the peoples in face of the united front of imperialist forces, because it nourishes bourgeois nationalist tendencies and may ultimtely lead to the loss of the socialist gains.

As they combine their effort in the building of a new society, the socialist states give active support to and extend their political, economic, and cultural cooperation with countries that have cast off colonial rule. They maintain—and are prepared to maintain—broad, mutually advantageous trade relations and cultural contacts with the capitalist countries.

The development of the world socialist system and of the world capitalist system is governed by diametrically opposed laws. The world capitalist system emerged and developed in fierce struggle between the countries composing it, through the subjection and exploitation of the weaker countries by the strong, through the enslavement of hundreds of millions of people, and the reduction of entire continents to the status of colonial appendages of the imperialist metropolitan countries. The formation and development of the world socialist system, on the other hand, proceeds on the basis of sovereignty and free will and in conformity with the fundamental interests of the working people of all the countries of that system.

Whereas the world capitalist system is governed by the law of uneven economic and political development that leads to conflicts between countries, the world socialist system is governed by opposite laws, which ensure the steady and balanced growth of the economies of all countries belonging to that system. Growth of production in a country belonging to the capitalist world deepens the contradictions between countries and intensifies competitive rivalries. The development of each socialist country, on the other hand, promotes the general progress and consolidation of the world socialist system as a whole. The economy of world capitalism develops at a slow rate, and goes through crises and upheavals. Typical of the economy of world socialism, on the other hand, are high and stable rates of growth and the common unintermittent economic progress of all socialist countries.

All the socialist countries make their contribution to the building and development of the world socialist system and the consolidation of its might. The existence of the Soviet Union greatly facilitates and accelerates the building of socialism in the People's Democracies. The Marxist-Leninist parties and the peoples of the socialist countries proceed from the fact that the successes of the world socialist system as a whole depend on the contribution and effort made by each country, and therefore consider the greatest possible development of the productive forces of their country an internationalist duty. The cooperation of the socialist countries enables each country to use its resources and develop its productive forces to the full and in the most rational manner. *A new type of international division of labor* is taking shape in the process of the economic, scientific and technical cooperation of the socialist countries, the coordination of their economic plans, the specialization and combination of production.

The establishment of the Union of Soviet Socialist Republics

and, later, of the world socialist system is the commencement of
the historical process of all-round association of the peoples.
With the disappearance of class antagonisms in the fraternal
family of socialist countries, national antagonisms also disappear.
The rapid cultural progress of the peoples of the socialist community is attended by a progressive mutual enrichment of the
national cultures and an active molding of the internationalist
features typical of man in socialist society.

The experience of the peoples of the world socialist community
has confirmed that their fraternal *unity and cooperation* conform
to the supreme national interests of each country. The strengthening of the unity of the world socialist system on the basis of
proletarian internationalism is an imperative condition for the
further progress of all its member countries.

The socialist system has to cope with certain difficulties, deriving chiefly from the fact that most of the countries in that
system had a medium or even low level of economic development
in the past, and also from the fact that world reaction is doing its
utmost to impede the building of socialism.

The experience of the Soviet Union and the People's Democracies has confirmed the accuracy of Lenin's thesis that the class
struggle does not disappear in the period of the building of socialism. The general trend of class struggle within the socialist
countries in conditions of successful socialist construction leads
to consolidation of the position of the socialist forces and weakens
the resistance of the remnants of the hostile classes. But this
development does not follow a straight line. Changes in the domestic or external situation may cause the class struggle to intensify in specific periods. This calls for constant vigilance in
order to frustrate in good time the designs of hostile forces within
and without, who persist in their attempts to undermine people's power and sow strife in the fraternal community of socialist
countries.

Nationalism is the chief political and ideological weapon
used by international reaction and the remnants of the domestic
reactionary forces against the unity of the socialist countries.
Nationalist sentiments and national narrow-mindedness do not
disappear automatically with the establishment of the socialist

system. Nationalist prejuidice and survivals of former national strife are a province in which resistance to social progress may be most protracted and stubborn, bitter and insidious.

The Communists consider it their prime duty to educate working people in a spirit of internationalism, socialist patriotism, and intolerance of all possible manifestations of nationalism and chauvinism. Nationalism is harmful to the common interests of the socialist community and, above all, the people of the country where it obtains, since isolation from the socialist camp holds up that country's development, deprives it of the advantages deriving from the world socialist system and encourages the imperialist powers to make the most of nationalist tendencies for their own ends. Nationalism can gain the upper hand only where it is not consistently combated. The Marxist-Leninist internationalist policy and determined efforts to wipe out the survivals of bourgeois nationalism and chauvinism are an important condition for the further consolidation of the socialist community. Yet while they oppose nationalism and national egoism, Communists always show utmost consideration for the national feelings of the masses.

The world socialist system is advancing steadfastly towards decisive victory in its economic competition with capitalism. It will shortly surpass the world capitalist system in aggregate industrial and agricultural production. Its influence on the course of social development in the interests of peace, democracy, and socialism is growing more and more.

The magnificent edifice of the new world being built by the heroic labors of the free peoples on vast areas of Europe and Asia is a prototype of the new society, of the future of all mankind.

IV. Crisis of World Capitalism

Imperialism has entered the period of decline and collapse. An inexorable process of decay has seized capitalism from top to bottom—its economic and political system, its politics and ideology. Imperialism has forever lost its power over the bulk of mankind. The main content, main trend, and main features of the historical development of mankind are being determined by the world socialist system, by the forces fighting against imperialism, for the socialist reorganization of society.

The First World War and the October Revolution ushered in the general crisis of capitalism. The second stage of this crisis developed at the time of the Second World War and the socialist revolutions that took place in a number of European and Asian countries. World capitalism has now entered a new, third stage of that crisis, the principal feature of which is that its development was not connected with a world war.

The breakaway from capitalism of more and more countries; the weakening of imperialist positions in the economic competition with socialism; the break-up of the imperialist colonial system; the intensification of imperialist contradictions with the development of state monopoly capitalism and the growth of militarism; the mounting internal instability and decay of capitalist economy evidenced by the increasing inability of capitalism to make full use of the productive forces (low rates of production growth, periodic crises, continuous undercapacity operation of production plant, and chronic unemployment); the mounting struggle between labor and capital; an acute intensification of contradictions within the world capitalist economy; an unprecedented growth of political reaction in all spheres, rejection of bourgeois freedoms and establishment of fascist and despotic regimes in a number of countries; and the profound crisis of bourgeois policy and ideology—all these are manifestations of the *general crisis of capitalism.*

In the imperialist stage *state monopoly capitalism* develops on an extensive scale. The emergence and growth of monopolies lead to the direct intervention of the state, in the interests of the financial oligarchy, in the process of capitalist reproduction. It is in the interests of the financial oligarchy that the bourgeois state institutes various types of regulation and resorts to the nationalization of some branches of the economy. World wars, economic crises, militarism, and political upheavals have accelerated the development of monopoly capitalism into state monopoly capitalism.

The oppression of finance capital keeps growing. Giant monopolies controlling the bulk of social production dominate the life of the nation. A handful of millionaires and multimillionaires wield arbitrary power over the entire wealth of the capitalist world and make the life of entire nations mere small change in their selfish deals. The financial oligarchy is getting fabulously rich. The state has become a committee for the management of the affairs of the monopoly bourgeoisie. The bureaucratization of the economy is rising steeply. State monopoly capitalism combines the strength of the monopolies and that of the state into a single mechanism whose purpose is to enrich the monopolies, suppress the working-class movement and the national liberation struggle, save the capitalist system, and launch aggressive wars.

The Right-wing Socialists and revisionists are making out state monopoly capitalism to be almost socialism. The facts give the lie to this contention. State monopoly capitalism does not change the nature of imperialism. Far from altering the position of the principal classes in the system of social production, it widens the rift between labor and capital, between the majority of the nation and the monopolies. Attempts at state regulation of the capitalist economy cannot eliminate competition and anarchy of production, cannot ensure the planned development of the economy on a nation-wide scale, because capitalist ownership and exploitation of wage labor remain the basis of production. The bourgeois theories of "crisis-free" and "planned" capitalism have been laid in the dust by the development of contemporary capitalist economy. The dialectics of state monopoly capitalism is such that instead of shoring up the capitalist system, as the bourgeoisie expects, it aggravates the contradictions of capitalism and undermines its foundations. State monopoly capitalism is the fullest material preparation for socialism.

The new phenomena in imperialist development corroborate the accuracy of Lenin's conclusions on the principal objective laws of capitalism in its final stage and on its increasing decay. Yet this decay does not signify complete stagnation, a palsy of its productive forces, and does not rule out growth of capitalist economy at particular times and in particular countries.

All in all, capitalism is increasingly impeding the development of the contemporary productive forces. Mankind is entering the period of a scientific and technical revolution bound up with the conquest of nuclear energy, space exploration, the development of chemistry, automation, and other major achievements of science and engineering. But the relations of production under capitalism are much too narrow for a scientific and technical revolution. Socialism alone is capable of effecting it and of applying its fruits in the interests of society.

Technical progress under the rule of monopoly capital is turning against the working class. By using new forms, the monopolies intensify the exploitation of the working class. Capitalist automation is robbing the worker of his daily bread. Unemployment is rising, the living standard is dropping. Technical progress is continuously throwing more sections of small producers overboard. Imperialism is using technical progress chiefly for military purposes. It is turning the achievements of human genius against humanity. As long as imperialism exists, mankind cannot feel secure about its future.

Modern capitalism has made the *market problem* extremely acute. Imperialism is incapable of solving it, because lag of effective demand behind growth of production is one of its objective laws. Moreover, it retards the industrial development of the underdeveloped countries. The world capitalist market is shrinking relative to the more rapidly expanding production capacity. It is partitioned by countless customs barriers and restrictive fences and split into exclusive currency and finance zones. An acute competitive struggle for markets, spheres of investment, and sources of raw materials is under way in the imperialist camp. It is becoming doubly acute since the territorial sphere of capitalist domination has been greatly narrowed.

Monopoly capital has, in the final analysis, doomed bourgeois society to low rates of production growth that in some countries barely keep ahead of the growth of population. A considerable part of the production plant stands idle, while millions of unemployed wait at the factory gates. Farm production is artificially restricted, although millions are underfed in the world.

People suffer want in material goods, but imperialism is squandering material resources and social labor on war preparations.

Abolition of the capitalist system in a large group of countries, the developing and strengthening of the world socialist system, the disintegration of the colonial system and the collapse of old empires, the commencing reorganization of the colonial economic structure in the newly-free countries, and the expanding economic connections between the latter and the socialist world —all these factors intensify *the crisis of the world capitalist economy*.

State monopoly capitalism stimulates militarism to an unheard-of degree. The imperialist countries maintain immense armed forces in peacetime. Military expenditures devour an ever-growing portion of the state budgets. The imperialist countries are turning into militarist, military-police states. Militarization pervades the life of bourgeois society.

While enriching some groups of the monopoly bourgeoisie, militarism leads to the exhaustion of nations, to the ruin of the peoples languishing under an excessive tax burden, mounting inflation, and a high cost of living. Within the lifetime of one generation imperialism plunged mankind into the abyss of two destructive world wars. In the First World War the imperialists annihilated ten million and crippled twenty million people. The Second World War claimed nearly fifty million human lives. In the course of these wars entire countries were ravaged, thousands of towns and villages were demolished, and the fruits of the labor of many generations were destroyed. The new war being hatched by the imperialists threatens mankind with unprecedented human losses and destruction. Even the preparations for it bring suffering and privation to millions of people.

The progress achieved in the development of the productive forces and the socialization of labor is being usurped by the contemporary capitalist state in the interests of the monopolies.

The monopoly bourgeoisie is a useless growth on the social organism, one unneeded in production. The industries are run by hired managers, engineers, and technicians. The monopolists lead a parasitical life and with their menials consume a substantial portion of the national income created by the toil of proletarians and peasants.

Fear of revolution, the successes of the socialist countries, and the pressure of the working-class movement compel the bourgeoisie to make partial concessions with respect to wages, labor conditions, and social security. But more often than not mounting prices and inflation reduce these concessions to nought. Wages lag behind the daily material and cultural requirements of the worker and his family, which grow as society develops. Even the relatively high standard of living in the small group of capitalistically developed countries rests upon the plunder of the Asian, African, and Latin American peoples, upon non-equivalent exchange, discrimination against female labor, brutal oppression of Negroes and immigrant workers, and also upon the intensified exploitation of the working people in those countries. The bourgeois myth of "full employment" has proved to be sheer mockery, for the working class is suffering continuously from mass unemployment and insecurity. In spite of some successes in the economic struggle, the condition of the working class in the capitalist world is deteriorating, on the whole.

The development of capitalism has dissipated the legend of the stability of small peasant farming once and for all. The monopolies have seized dominant positions in agriculture as well. Millions of farmers and peasants are being driven off the land, and their farms are being brought under the hammer. Small farms survive at the price of appalling hardships, the peasants' underconsumption, and excessive labor. The peasantry is groaning under the burden of mounting taxes and debts. Agrarian crises are bringing ever greater ruin to the countryside. Unspeakable want and poverty fall to the lot of the peasantry in the colonial and dependent countries; it suffers the dual oppression of the landlords and the monopoly bourgeoisie.

The monopolies are also ruining small urban proprietors. Handicrafts are going under. Small-scale industrial and commercial enterprises are fully dependent upon the monopolies.

Life has fully confirmed the Marxist thesis of increasing proletarianization in capitalist society. The expropriated masses have no other prospect of acquiring property than the revolutionary establishment of the social ownership of means of production, that is, making them the property of the whole people.

The uneven development of capitalism alters the balance of forces between countries and makes the contradictions between them more acute. The economic and with it the political and military center of imperialism, has shifted from Europe to the United States. U.S. monopoly capital, gorged on war profits and the arms race, has seized the most important sources of raw materials, the markets and the spheres of investment, has built up a unique kind of colonial empire and become the biggest *international exploiter*. Taking cover behind spurious professions of freedom and democracy, U.S. imperialism is in effect performing the function of *world gendarme,* supporting reactionary dictatorial regimes and decayed monarchies, opposing democratic, revolutionary changes and launching aggressions against peoples fighting for independence.

The U.S. monopoly bourgeoisie is the mainstay of international reaction. It has assumed the role of "savior" of capitalism. The U.S. financial tycoons are engineering a "holy alliance" of imperialists and founding aggressive military blocs. American troops and war bases are located at the most important points of the capitalist world.

But the facts reveal the utter incongruity of the U.S. imperialist claims to world domination. Imperialism has proved incapable of stemming the socialist and national liberation revolutions. The hopes which American imperialism pinned on its atomic weapons monopoly fell through. The United States has not been able to retain its share in the economy of the capitalist world, although it is still capitalism's chief economic, financial, and military force. The United States, the strongest capitalist power, is past its zenith and has entered the stage of decline, Imperialist countries such as Great Britain, France, Germany, and Japan have also lost their former power.

The basic contradiction of the contemporary world, that between socialism and imperialism, does not eliminate the *deep contradictions* rending the capitalist world. The aggressive military blocs founded under the aegis of the United States are time and again faced with crises. The international state monopoly organizations springing up under the motto of "integration," the mitigation of the market problem, are in reality new forms of the redivision of the world capitalist market and are becoming seats of acute strain and conflict.

The contradictions between the principal imperialist powers are growing deeper. The economic rehabilitation of the imperialist countries defeated in the Second World War leads to the revival of the old and the emergence of new knots of imperialist rivalry and conflict. The Anglo-American, Franco-American, Franco-West German, American-West German, Anglo-West German, Japanese-American, and other contradictions are becoming especially acute. Fresh contradictions will inevitably arise and grow in the imperialist camp.

The American monopolies and their British and French allies are openly assisting the West German imperialists who are cynically advocating aggressive aims of revenge and preparing a war against the socialist countries and other European states. A dangerous center of aggression, imperilling the peace and security of all peoples, is being revived in the heart of Europe. In the Far East the American monopolies are reviving Japanese militarism, which is in a certain way dependent on them. This constitutes another dangerous hotbed of war threatening the countries of Asia and, above all, the socialist countries.

The interests of the small group of imperialist powers are incompatible with the interests of all other countries, the interests of all peoples. Deep-rooted antagonism divides the imperialist countries from the countries that have won national independence and those that are fighting for their liberation.

Contemporary capitalism is inimical to the vital interests and progressive aspirations of all mankind. Capitalism with its exploitation of man by man, with its chauvinist and racist ideology, with its moral degradation, its rampage of profiteering, corruption, and crime is defiling society, the family, and man.

The bourgeois system came into being with the alluring slogans of liberty, equality, fraternity. But the bourgeoisie made use of these slogans merely to elbow out the feudal gentry and to assume power. Instead of equality a new gaping abyss of social and economic inequality appeared. Not fraternity but ferocious class struggle reigns in bourgeois society.

Monopoly capital is revealing its reactionary, anti-democratic substance more and more strikingly. It does not tolerate even the former bourgeois democratic freedoms, although it proclaims them hypocritically. In the current stage of historical development it is getting harder for the bourgeoisie to propagate slogans of equality and liberty. The upswing of the international labor movement restricts the maneuvers of finance capital. Finance capital can no longer squash the revolutionary sentiments of the masses and cope with the inexorably growing revolutionary, anti-imperialist movement by means of the old slogans and by bribing the labor bureaucracy.

Having taken full possession of the principal material values, monopoly capital refuses to share political power with anyone. It has established a dictatorship, the dictatorship of the minority over the majority, the dictatorship of the capitalist monopolies over society. The ideologists of imperialism hide the dictatorship of monopoly capital behind specious slogans of freedom and democracy. They declare the imperialist powers to be countries of the "free world" and represent the ruling bourgeois circles as opponents of all dictatorship. In reality, however, freedom in the imperialist world signifies nothing but freedom to exploit the working class, the working people, not only at home, but in all other countries that fall under the iron heel of the monopolies.

The bourgeoisie gives extensive publicity to the allegedly democratic nature of its election laws, singing special praise to its multi-party system and the possibility of nominating many candidates. In reality, however, the monopolists deprive the masses of the opportunity to express their will and elect genuine champions of their interests. Being in control of such potent means as capital, the press, radio, cinema, television, and using their henchmen in the trade unions and other mass organizations, they mislead the masses and impose their own candidates upon the electorate. The different bourgeois parties are usually no more than different factions of the ruling bourgeoisie.

The dictatorship of the bourgeoisie also grossly violates the will of the electorate. Whenever the bourgeoisie sees that the working people are likely, by using their constitutional rights, to elect a considerable number of the champions of their interests to the legislative organs, it brazenly alters the election system and arbitrarily limits the number of working people's representatives in parliament.

The financial oligarchy resorts to the establishment of fascist regimes, banking on the army, police, and gendarmerie as a last refuge from the people's wrath, especially when the masses try to make use of their democratic rights, albeit curtailed, to uphold their interests and end the all-pervading power of the monopolies. Although the vicious German and Italian fascism has crashed, fascist regimes still survive in some countries and fascism is being revived in new forms in others.

Thus, *the world imperialist system is rent by deep-rooted and acute contradictions.* The antagonism of labor and capital, the contradictions between the people and the monopolies, growing militarism, the break-up of the colonial system, the contradictions between the imperialist countries, conflicts and contradictions between the young national states and the old colonial powers, and—most important of all—the rapid growth of world socialism, are sapping and destroying imperialism, leading to its weakening and collapse.

Not even nuclear weapons can protect the monopoly bourgeoisie from the unalterable course of historical development. Mankind has learned the true face of capitalism. Hundreds of millions of people see that capitalism is a system of economic anarchy and periodical crises, chronic unemployment, poverty of the masses, and indiscriminate waste of productive forces, a system constantly fraught with the danger of war. Mankind does not want to, and will not, tolerate the historically outdated capitalist system.

V. The International Revolutionary Movement of the Working Class

The international revolutionary movement of the working class has achieved epoch-making victories. *Its chief gain is the world socialist system.* The example of victorious socialism is revolutionizing the minds of the working people of the capitalist world; it inspires them to fight against imperialism and greatly facilitates their struggle.

Social forces that are to ensure the victory of socialism are taking shape, multiplying and becoming steeled in the womb of capitalist society. A new contingent of the world proletariat— the young working-class movement of the newly-free, dependent and colonial countries of Asia, Africa, and Latin America—has entered the world arena. Marxist-Leninist parties have arisen and grown. They are becoming a universally recognized national force enjoying ever greater prestige and followed by large sections of the working people.

The international revolutionary movement has accumulated vast experience in the struggle against imperialism and its placemen in the ranks of the working class. It has become more mature ideologically and possesses great organized strength and a militantly dynamic spirit. The trade union movement, which unites vast masses of working people, is playing an increasing role.

The capitalist countries are continuously shaken by class battles, Militant actions of the working class in defense of its economic and political interests are growing in number. The working class and all working people have frequently imperilled the class rule of the bourgeoisie. In an effort to maintain its power, the finance oligarchy, in addition to methods of suppression, uses diverse ways of deceiving and corrupting the working class and its organizations, and of splitting the trade union movement on a national and international scale. It bribes the top stratum of trade unions, cooperatives and other organizations and swells the labor bureaucracy, to which it allots lucrative positions in industry, the municipal bodies, and the government apparatus. Anti-communist and anti-labor legislation, the banning of Communist parties, wholesale dismissal of Communists and other progressive workers, blacklisting in industry, "loyalty" screening of employees, police reprisals against the democratic press, and the suppression of strikes by military force have all become routine methods of action for the governments of the imperialist bourgeoisie in its efforts to preserve its dictatorship.

The reactionary forces in individual capitalist countries can no longer cope with the growing forces of democracy and socialism. Struggle and competition between the capitalist states do not preclude, however, a certain unity among them in the face of the increasing strength of socialism and the working-class movement. The imperialists form reactionary alliances; they enter into mutual agreements and set up military blocs and bases spearheaded not only against the socialist countries, but also against the revolutionary working-class and national liberation movement. The reactionary bourgeoisie in a number of European states have in peacetime opened the doors of their countries to foreign troops.

The bourgeoisie seeks to draw definite lessons from the October Revolution and the victories of socialism. It is using new methods to cover up the ulcers and vices of the capitalist system. Although all these methods render the activities of the revolutionary forces in the capitalist countries more difficult, they cannot reduce the contradictions between labor and capital.

The world situation today is more favorable to the working-class movement. The achievements of the USSR and the world socialist system as a whole, the deepening crisis of world capitalism, the growing influence of the Communist parties among the masses, and the ideological breakdown of reformism have brought about a substantial change in the conditions of class struggle that is to the advantage of the working people. Even in those countries where reformism still holds strong positions, appreciable shifts to the Left are taking place in the working-class movement.

In the new historical situation, the working class of many countries can, even before capitalism is overthrown, compel the bourgeoisie to carry out measures that transcend ordinary reforms and are of vital importance to the working class and the progress of its struggle for the victory of the revolution, for socialism, as well as to the majority of the nation. By uniting the democratic and peace-loving forces, the working class can make ruling circles cease preparations for a new world war, renounce the policy of starting local wars, and use the economy for peaceful purposes. By uniting the working people, the masses, the working class can beat back the offensive of fascist reaction and bring about the implementation of a national program for peace, national independence, democratic rights, and a certain improvement of the living conditions of the people.

The capitalist monopolies are the chief enemy of the working class. They are also the chief enemy of the peasants, handicraftsmen, and other small urban proprietors, of most office workers and intellectuals, and even of a section of the middle capitalists.

The working class directs its main blow against the capitalist monopolies. All the main sections of a nation have a vital interest in abolishing the unlimited power of the monopolies. This makes it possible to unite all the democratic movements opposing the oppression of the finance oligarchy in a mighty *anti-monopoly torrent*.

The proletariat advances a program for combating the power of the monopolies with due regard to the present as well as the future interests of its allies. It advocates broad nationalization on terms most favorable to the people. It backs the peasants' demands for radical land reforms and works for the realization of the slogan, "The land to those who till it."

The proletariat, together with other sections of the people, wages a resolute struggle for broad democracy. It mobilizes the masses for effective action against the policy of the finance oligarchy, which strives to abolish democratic freedoms, restrict the power of parliament, revise the constitution with the aim of establishing the personal power of monopoly placemen, and to go over from the parliamentary system to some variety of fascism.

It is in this struggle that the alliance of the working class and all working people is shaped. The working class unites the peasantry, its chief ally, to combat the survivals of feudalism and monopoly domination. Large sections of the office workers and a considerable section of the intelligentsia, whom capitalism reduces to the status of proletarians and who realize the need of changes in the social sphere, become allies of the working class.

General democratic struggles against the monopolies do not

delay the socialist revolution but bring it nearer. *The struggle for democracy is a component of the struggle for socialism.* The more profound the democratic movement, the higher becomes the level of the political consciousness of the masses and the more clearly they see that only socialism clears for them the way to genuine freedom and well-being. In the course of this struggle, Right socialist, reformist illusions are dispelled and a political army of the socialist revolution is brought into being.

Socialist revolutions, anti-imperialist national liberation revolutions, people's democratic revolutions, broad peasant movements, popular struggles to overthrow fascist and other despotic regimes, and general democratic movements against national oppression—all these merge in a single world-wide revolutionary process undermining and destroying capitalism.

The proletarian revolution in any country, being part of the world socialist revolution, is accomplished by the working class of that country and the masses of its people. The revolution is not made to order. It cannot be imposed on the people from without. It results from the profound internal and international contradictions of capitalism. The victorious proletariat cannot impose any "felicity" on another people without thereby undermining its own victory.

Together with the other Marxist-Leninist parties, the Communist Party of the Soviet Union regards it as its internationalist duty to call on the peoples of all countries to rally, muster all internal forces, take vigorous action, and drawing on the might of the world socialist system, forestall or firmly repel imperialist interference in the affairs of the people of any country risen in revolt and thereby prevent imperialist export of counter-revolution. It will be easier to prevent export of counter-revolution if the working people, defending the national sovereignty of their country, strive to bring about the abolition of foreign military bases on their territory and to make their country dissociate itself from aggressive military blocs.

Communists have never held that the road to revolution lies necessarily through wars between countries. Socialist revolution is not necessarily connected with war. Although both world wars, which were started by the imperialists, culminated in socialist revolutions, revolutions are quite feasible without war. The great objectives of the working class can be realized without world war. Today the conditions for this are more favorable than ever.

The working class and its vanguard—the Marxist-Leninist parties—seek to accomplish the socialist revolution *by peaceful means*. This would meet the interests of the working class and the people as a whole, it would accord with the national interests of the country.

In the conditions prevaling at present, in some capitalist countries the working class, headed by its forward detachment, has an opportunity to unite the bulk of the nation, win state power without a civil war and achieve the transfer of the basic means of production to the people upon the basis of a working-class and popular front and other possible forms of agreement and political cooperation between different parties and democratic organizations. The working class, supported by the majority of the people and firmly repelling opportunist elements incapable of renouncing the policy of compromise with the capitalists and landlords, can defeat the reactionary, anti-popular forces, win a solid majority in parliament, transform it from a tool serving the class interests of the bourgeoisie into an instrument serving the working people, launch a broad mass struggle outside parliament, smash the resistance of the reactionary forces, and provide the necessary conditions for a peaceful socialist revolution. This can be done only by extending and continuously developing the class struggle of the workers and peasants and the middle strata of the urban population against big monopoly capital and reaction, for far-reaching social reforms, for peace and socialism.

Where the exploiting classes resort to violence against the people, the possibility of a *non-peaceful transition to socialism* should be borne in mind. Leninism maintains, and historical experience confirms, that the ruling classes do not yield power of their own free will. Hence, the degree of bitterness of the class struggle and the forms it takes will depend not so much on the proletariat as on the strength of the reactionary groups' resistance to the will of the overwhelming majority of the people, and on the use of force by these groups at a particular stage of the struggle for socialism. In each particular country the actual applicability of one method of transition to socialism or the other depends on concrete historical conditions.

It may well be that as the forces of socialism grow, as the working-class movement gains strength, and as the positions of capitalism are weakend, there will arise in certain countries a situation in which it will be preferable for the bourgeoisie, as Marx and Lenin foresaw, to agree to the basic means of production being purchased from it and for the proletariat to "pay off" the bourgeoisie.

The success of the struggle which the working class wages for the victory of the revolution will depend on how well the working class and its party master the use of *all forms* of struggle—peaceful and non-peaceful, parliamentary and extra-parliamentary—and how well they are prepared for any swift and sudden replacement of one form of struggle by another form of struggle. While the principal law-governed processes of the socialist revolution are common to all countries, the diversity of the national pecularities and traditions that have arisen in the course of history creates specific conditions for the revolutionary process, the variety of forms and rates of the proletariat's advent to power. This predetermines the possibility and necessity, in a number of countries, of *transition stages* in the struggle for the dictatorship of the proletariat, and a *variety of forms* of political organization of the society building socialism. But whatever the form in which the transition from capitalism to socialism is effected, that transition can come about only through revolution. However varied the forms of a new, people's state power in the period of socialist construction, their essence will be the same—*dictatorship of the proletariat*, which represents genuine democracy, democracy for the working people.

A bourgeois republic, however democratic, however hallowed by slogans purporting to express the will of the people or nation as a whole, or extra-class will, inevitably remains in practice—owing to the existence of private capitalist ownership of the means of production—a dictatorship of the bourgeoisie, a machine for the exploitation and suppression of the vast majority of the working people by a handful of capitalists. In contrast to the bourgeoisie, which conceals the class character of the state.

the working class does not deny the class character of the state.

The dictatorship of the proletariat is a dictatorship of the over-whelming majority over the minority; it is directed against the exploiters, against the oppression of peoples and nations, and is aimed at abolishing all exploitation of man by man. The dictator-ship of the proletariat expresses not only the interests of the work-ing class, but also those of all working people; its chief content is not violence but creation, the building of a new, socialist society, and the defense of its gains against the enemies of socialism.

Overcoming the split in its ranks is an important condition for the working class to fulfil its historic mission. No bastion of impe-rialism can withstand a closely-knit working class that exercises unity of action. The Communist parties favor cooperation with the Social-Democratic parties not only in the struggle for peace, for better living conditions for the working people, and for the preservation and extension of their democratic rights and free-doms, but also in the struggle to win power and build a socialist society.

At the same time Communists criticize the ideological positions and Right-wing opportunist practice of Social-Democracy and expose the Right Social-Democratic leaders who have sided openly with the bourgeoisie and renounced the traditional socialist demands of the working class.

The Communist parties are the vanguard of the world rev-olutionary movement. They have demonstrated the vitality of Marxism-Leninism and their ability not only to propagate the great ideals of scientific communism, but also to put them into practice. Today the international Communist movement is so powerful that the combined forces of reaction cannot crush it.

The Communist movement grows and becomes steeled as it fights against various opportunist trends. Revisionism, Right opportunism, which is a reflection of bourgeois influence, is the chief danger within the Communist movement today. The revi-sionists, who mask their renunciation of Marxism with talk about the necessity of taking account of the latest developments in society and the class struggle, in effect play the role of peddlers of bourgeois-reformist ideology within the Communist movement. They seek to rob Marxism-Leninism of its revolutionary spirit, to undermine the faith which the working class and all working people have in socialism, to disarm and disorganize them in their struggle against imperialism. The revisionists deny the historical necessity of socialist revolution and of the dictatorship of the proletariat. They deny the leading role of the Marxist-Leninist party, undermine the foundations of proletarian internationalism, and drift to nationalism. The ideology of revisionism is most fully embodied in the program of the League of Communists of Yugoslavia.

Another danger is dogmatism and sectarianism, which cannot be reconciled with a creative development of revolutionary theory, which lead to the dissociation and isolation of Communists from the masses, doom them to passive expectation or incite them to Leftist adventurist actions in the revolutionary struggle, and hinder a correct appraisal of the changing situation and the use of new opportunities for the benefit of the working class and all democratic forces. Dogmatism and sectarianism, unless steadfastly combated, can also become the chief danger at particular stages in the development of individual parties.

The Communist Party of the Soviet Union holds that an uncompromising struggle against revisionism, dogmatism and sectarianism, against all departures from Leninism, is a necessary condition for the further strengthening of the unity of the world Communist movement and for the consolidation of the socialist camp.

The Communist parties are independent and they shape their policies with due regard to the specific conditions prevailing in their own countries. They base relations between themselves on equality and the principles of proletarian internationalism. They coordinate their actions, consciously and of their own free will, as components of a single international army of labor. The Communist Party of the Soviet Union, like all the other Communist parties, regards it as its internationalist duty to abide by the appraisals and conclusions which the fraternal parties have reached jointly concerning their common tasks in the struggle against imperialism, for peace, democracy and socialism, and by the Declaration and the Statement adopted by the Communist parties at their international meetings.

Vigorous defense of the unity of the world Communist movement in line with the principles of Marxism-Leninism and proletarian internationalism, and the prevention of any action likely
to disrupt that unity are an essential condition for victory in the
struggle for national independence, democracy and peace, for
the successful accomplishment of the tasks of the socialist revolution, for the construction of socialism and communism.

The CPSU will continue to concentrate its efforts on strengthening the unity and cohesion of the ranks of the great army of
Communists of all countries.

VI. The National Liberation Movement

The world is experiencing a period of stormy national liberation revolutions. Imperialism suppressed the national independence and freedom of the majority of the peoples and put the
fetters of brutal colonial slavery on them, but *the rise of socialism marks the advent of the era of emancipation of the
oppressed peoples.* A powerful wave of national liberation revolutions is sweeping away the colonial system and undermining
the foundations of imperialism. Young sovereign states have
arisen, or are arising, in one-time colonies or semi-colonies. Their
peoples have entered a new period of development. Thy have
emerged as makers of a new life and as active participants in
world politics, as a revolutionary force destroying imperialism.

But the struggle is not yet over. The peoples who are throwing off the shackles of colonialism have attained different degrees
of freedom. Many of them, having established national states, are
striving for economic and durable political independence. The
peoples of those formally independent countries that in reality
depend on foreign monopolies politically and economically are
rising to fight against imperialism and reactionary pro-imperialist regimes. The peoples who have not yet cast off the chains
of colonial slavery are conducting a heroic struggle against their
foreign enslavers.

The young sovereign states do not belong either to the system of imperialist states or to the system of socialist states. But the overwhelming majority of them have not yet broken free from world capitalist economy even though they occupy a special place in it. They constitute that part of the world which is still being exploited by the capitalist monopolies. As long as they do not put an end to their economic dependence on imperialism, they will be playing the role of a "world countryside," and will remain objects of semi-colonial exploitation.

The existence of the world socialist system and the weakening of imperialism offer the peoples of the newly-free countries the prospect of a national renascence, of ending age-long backwardness and poverty, and achieving economic independence

The interests of a nation call for the eradication of the remnants of colonialism, the elimination of the roots of imperialist power, the ousting of foreign monopolies, the founding of a national industry, the abolition of the feudal system and its survivals, the implementation of radical land reforms with the participation of the entire peasantry and in its interests, the pursuit of an independent foreign policy of peace, the democratization of the life of society, and the strengthening of political independence. All patriotic and progressive forces of the nation are interested in the solution of national problems. That is the basis on which they can be united.

Foreign capital will retreat only before a broad union of patriotic, democratic forces pursuing an anti-imperialist policy. The pillars of feudalism will crumble only under the impact of a general democratic movement. Only far-reaching agrarian reforms and a broad peasant movement can sweep away the remnants of medievalism that fetter the development of the productive forces, and solve the acute food problem that faces the peoples of Asia, Africa, and Latin America. Political independence can be made secure only by a people that has won democratic rights and freedoms and is taking an active part in governing the state.

Consistent struggle against imperialism is a paramount condition for the solution of national tasks. Imperialism seeks to retain one-time colonies and semi-colonies within the system of capitalist economy and perpetuate their underprivileged position in it. *U.S. imperialism is the chief bulwark of modern colonialism.*

The imperialists are using new methods and new forms to maintain colonial exploitation of the peoples. They resort to whatever means they can (colonial wars, military blocs, conspiracies, terrorism, subversion, economic pressure, bribery) to control the newly-free countries and to reduce the independence they have won to mere form, or to deprive them of that independence. Under the guise of "aid," they are trying to retain their old positions in those countries and capture new ones, to extend their social basis, lure the national bourgeoisie to their side, implant military despotic regimes, and put obedient puppets in power. Using the poisoned weapon of national and tribal strife, the imperialists seek to split the ranks of the national liberation movement; reactionary groups of the local exploiting classes play the role of allies of imperalism.

Imperialism thus remains the chief enemy and the chief obstacle to the solution of the national problems facing the young sovereign states and all dependent countries.

A national liberation revolution does not end with the winning of political independence. Independence will be unstable and will become fictitious unless the revolution brings about radical changes in the social and economic spheres and solves the pressing problems of national rebirth.

The working class is the most consistent fighter for the consummation of this revolution, for national interests and social progress. As industry develops, its ranks will swell and its role on the socio-political scene will increase. The alliance of the working class and the peasantry is the fundamental condition for the success of the struggle to carry out far-reaching democratic changes and achieve economic and social progress. This alliance must form the core of a broad national front. The extent to which the national bourgeoisie will take part in the anti-imperialist and anti-feudal struggle will depend in considerable measure on the solidity of the alliance of the working class and the peasantry. The national front embraces the working class, the peasantry, the national bourgeoisie, and the democratic intelligentsia.

In many countries, the liberation movement of the peoples that have awakened proceeds under the flag of nationalism. Marxists-Leninists draw a distinction between the nationalism of the oppressed nations and that of the oppressor nations. The nationalism of an oppressed nation contains a *general democratic element* directed against oppression, and Communists support it because they consider it historically justified at a given stage. That element finds expression in the striving of the oppressed peoples to free themselves from imperialist oppression, to gain national independence, and bring about a national renascence. But the nationalism of an oppressed nation has yet another aspect, one expressing the ideology and interests of the reactionary exploiting top stratum.

The national bourgeoisie is dual in character. In modern conditions the national bourgeoisie in those colonial, one-tme colonial and dependent countries where it is not connected with the imperialist circles is objectively interested in accomplishing the basic tasks of an anti-imperialist and anti-feudal revolution. Its progressive role and its ability to participate in the solution of pressing national problems are, therefore, not yet spent.

But as the contradictions between the working people and the propertied classes grow and the class struggle inside the country becomes more acute, the national bourgeoisie shows an increasing inclination to compromise with imperialism and domestic reaction.

The development of the countries which have won their freedom may be a complex multi-stage process. By virtue of varying historical and socio-economic conditions in the newly-free countries, the revolutionary effort of the masses will impart many distinctive features to the forms and rates of their social progress.

One of the basic questions confronting these peoples is which road of development the countries that have freed themselves from colonial tyranny are to take, whether the capitalist road or the non-capitalist.

What can capitalism bring them?

Capitalism is the road of suffering for the people. It will not ensure rapid economic progress nor eliminate poverty; social inequality will increase. The capitalist development of the countryside will ruin the peasantry still more. The workers will be fated either to engage in back-breaking labor to enrich the capitalists, or to swell the ranks of the disinherited army of the unemployed. The petty bourgeoisie will be crushed in competition with big capital. The benefits of culture and education will remain out of reach of the people. The intelligentsia will be compelled to sell its talent.

What can socialism bring the peoples?

Socialism is the road to freedom and happiness for the peoples. It ensures rapid economic and cultural progress. It transforms a backward country into an industrial country within the lifetime of one generation and not in the course of centuries. Planned socialist economy is an economy of progress and prosperity by its very nature. Abolition of the exploitation of man by man does away with social inequality. Unemployment disappears completely. Socialism provides all peasants with land, helps them to develop farming, combines their labor efforts in voluntary cooperatives and puts modern agricultural machinery and agronomy at their disposal. Peasant labor is made more productive and the land is made more fertile. Socialism provides a high material and cultural standard of living for the working class and all working people. Socialism lifts the people out of darkness and ignorance and gives them access to modern culture. The intelligentsia is offered ample opportunities for creative effort for the benefit of the people.

It is for the peoples themselves to decide which road they will choose. In view of the present balance of the world forces and the actual feasibility of powerful support from the world socialist system, the peoples of the former colonies can decide this question in their own interest. Their choice will depend on the balance of the class forces. The non-capitalist road of development is ensured by the struggle of the working class and the masses of the people, by the general democratic movement, and meets the interests of the absolute majority of the nation.

The establishment and development of *national democracies* opens vast prospects for the peoples of the economically underdeveloped countries. The political basis of a national democracy is a bloc of all the progressive, patriotic forces fighting to win complete national independence and broad democracy, and to consummate the anti-imperialist, anti-feudal, democratic revolution.

A steady growth of the class and national consciousness of the masses is a characteristic of the present stage of social development. The imperialists persist in distorting the idea of national sovereignty, in emasculating it of its main content, and in using it as a means of fomenting national egoism, implanting a spirit of national exclusiveness and increasing national antagonisms. The democratic forces establish the idea of national sovereignty in the name of equality for the peoples, of their mutual trust, friendship and assistance and of closer relations between them, in the name of social progress. The idea of national sovereignty in its democratic sense becomes more and more firmly established; it acquires increasing significance and becomes an important factor in the progressive development of society.

The Communist parties are steadfastly carrying on an active struggle to consummate the anti-imperialist, anti-feudal, democratic revolution, to establish a state of national democracy and achieve social progress. *The Communists' aims are in keeping with the supreme interests of the nation.* The attempts of reactionary circles to disrupt the national front under the guise of anti-communism and their persecution of Communists lead to the weakening of the national liberation movement and run counter to the national interests of the peoples; they imperil the gains achieved.

The national states become ever more active as an independent force on the world scene; objectively, this force is in the main a *progressive, revolutionary, and anti-imperialist force.* The countries and peoples that are now free from colonial oppression are to play a prominent part in the prevention of a new world war— the focal problem of today. The time is past when imperialism could freely use the manpower and material resources of those countries in its predatory wars. The time has come when the peoples of those countries, breaking the resistance of the reactionary circles and those connected with the colonialists, and overcoming the vacillation of the national bourgeoisie, can put their resources at the service of universal security and become a new bulwark of peace. This is what their own fundamental interests and the interests of all peoples demand.

The joining of the efforts of the newly-free peoples and of the peoples of the socialist countries in the struggle against the war danger is a cardinal factor of world peace. This mighty front, which expresses the will and strength of two-thirds of mankind, can force the imperialist aggressors to retreat.

The socialist countries are sincere and true friends of peoples fighting for their liberation and of those that have freed themselves from imperialist tyranny, and render them all-round support. They stand for the abolition of all forms of colonial oppression and vigorously promote the strengthening of the sovereignty of the states rising on the ruins of colonial empires.

The CPSU considers fraternal alliance with the peoples who have thrown off the colonial or semi-colonial yoke to be a cornerstone of its international policy. This alliance is based on the common vital interests of world socialism and the world national liberation movement. The CPSU regards it as its internationalist duty to assist the peoples who have set out to win and strengthen their national independence, all peoples who are fighting for the complete abolition of the colonial system.

VII. The Struggle Against Bourgeois and Reformist Ideology

A grim struggle is going on between two ideologies—communist and bourgeois—in the world today. This struggle is a reflection, in the spiritual life of mankind, of the historic process of transition from capitalism to socialism.

The new historical epoch has brought the revolutionary world outlook of the proletariat a genuine triumph. Marxism-Leninism has gripped the minds of progressive mankind.

Bourgeois doctrines and schools have failed in the test of history. They have been and still are unable to furnish scientific answers to the questions posed by life. The bourgeoisie is no longer in a position to put forward ideas that will induce the masses to follow it. More and more people in the capitalist countries are renouncing the bourgeois world outlook. *Bourgeois ideology is experiencing a grave crisis.*

A revolutionary change in the minds of vast masses is a long and complex process. The more victories the world socialist system achieves, the deeper the crisis of world capitalism and the sharper the class struggle, the more important becomes the role of Marxist-Leninist ideas in unifying and mobilizing the masses to fight for communism. The ideological struggle is a most important element of the class struggle of the proletariat.

Imperialist reaction mobilizes every possible means to exert ideological influence on the masses as it attempts to denigrate communism and its noble ideas and to defend capitalism. The chief ideological and political weapon of imperialism is *anti-communism,* which consists mainly in slandering the socialist system and distorting the policy and objectives of the Communist parties and Marxist-Leninst theory. Under the false slogans of anti-communism, imperialist reaction persecutes and hounds all that is progressive and revolutionary; it seeks to split the ranks of the working people and to paralyze the proletarians' will to fight. Rallied to this black banner today are all the enemies of social progress: the finance oligarchy and the military, the fascists and reactionary clericals, the colonialists and landlords and all the ideological and political supporters of imperialist reaction. Anti-communism is a reflection of the extreme decadence of bourgeois ideology.

The defenders of the bourgeois system, seeking to keep the masses in spiritual bondage, invent new "theories" designed to mask the exploiting character of the bourgeois system and to embellish capitalism. They assert that modern capitalism has changed its nature, that it has become "people's capitalism" in which property is "diffused" and capital becomes "democratic," that classes and class contradictions are disappearing, that "incomes are being equalized" and economic crises eliminated. In reality, however, the development of modern capitalism confirms the accuracy of the Marxist-Leninist theory of the growing contradictions and antagonisms in capitalist society and of the aggravation of the class struggle within it.

The advocates of the bourgeois state call it a *"welfare state."* They propagate the illusion that the capitalist state opposes monopolies and can achieve social harmony and universal well-being. But the masses see from their own experience that the bourgeois state is an obedient tool of the monopolies and that the vaunted "welfare" is welfare for the magnates of finance capital, and suffering and torture for hundreds of millions of working men.

The "theoreticians" of anti-communism describe the imperialist countries as the "free world." In reality the "free world" is a world of exploitation and lack of rights, a world where human dignity and national honor are trampled underfoot, a world of obscurantism and political reaction, of rabid militarism and of bloody reprisals against the working people.

Monopoly capital engenders *fascist ideology*—the ideology of chauvinism and racism. Fascism in power is an overt terroristic dictatorship of the most reactionary, most chauvinistic, and most imperialist elements of finance capital. Fascism begins everywhere and always with vicious anti-communism to isolate and rout the parties of the working class, to split the forces of the proletariat and defeat them piecemeal, and then to do away with all the other democratic parties and organizations and turn the people into the blind tool of the policy of the capitalist monopolies. Fascism strikes first of all at the Communist parties since they are the most consistent, staunch, and incorruptible defenders of the interests of the working class and all working people.

Imperialist reaction makes extensive use of *chauvinism and racism* to incite nationalist and racial conflicts, persecute entire nationalities and races (anti-Semitism, racial discrimination against Negroes and the peoples of the underdeveloped countries), blunt the class consciousness of the working people and divert the proletariat and its allies from the class struggle.

Clericalism is acquiring ever greater importance in the political and ideological arsenal of imperialism. The clericals do not confine themselves to using the Church and its ramified machinery. They now have their own big political parties which are in power in many capitalist countries. By setting up its own trade union, youth, women's and other organizations clericalism splits the ranks of the working class and all working people. The monopolies lavishly subsidize clerical parties and organizations, which exploit the religious sentiments of the working peoples and their superstitions and prejudices.

Bourgeois ideology assumes a variety of forms and uses the most diverse methods and means of deceiving the working people. But they all boil down to the same thing—defense of the declining capitalist system. The ideas running through the political and economic theories of the modern bourgeoisie, through its philosophy and sociology, through its ethics and esthetics, substantiate monopoly domination, justify exploitation, defame social property and collectivism, glorify militarism and war, whitewash colonialism and racism, and foment enmity and hatred among the peoples.

Anti-communism is becoming the main instrument of reaction in its struggle against the democratic forces of Asia, Africa, and Latin America. It is the meeting ground of imperialist ideology and the ideology of the feudal, pro-imperialist elements and the reactionary groups of the bourgeoisie of the countries which have gained their freedom from colonial tyranny.

The anti-popular circles of those countries seek to tone down the general democratic content of nationalism, to play up its reactionary aspect, to push aside the democratic forces of the nation, to prevent social progress, and to hinder the spread of scientific socialism. At the same time they advance theories of "socialism of the national type," propagate socio-philosophical doctrines that are, as a rule, so many variations of the petty-bourgeois illusion of socialism, an illusion which rules out the class struggle. These theories mislead the people, hamper the development of the national liberation movement, and imperil its gains.

National democratic, anti-imperialist ideas are becoming widespread in the countries which have liberated themselves from colonial oppression. The Communists and other proponents of these ideas patiently explain to the masses the untenability of the illusion that national independence and social progress are possible without a determined struggle against imperialism and internal reaction. They come out actively against chauvinism and other manifestations of reactionary ideology, which justifies despotic regimes and the suppression of democracy. At the same time the Communists act as exponents of the socialist ideology, rallying the masses under the banner of scientific socialism.

The ideological struggle of the imperialist bourgeoisie is spearheaded primarily against the working class and its Marxist-Leninist parties. Social-Democratism in the working-class movement and revisionism in the Communist movement reflect the bourgeois influence on the working class.

The contemporary Right-wing Social-Democrats are the most important ideological and political prop of the bourgeoisie within the working-class movement. They eclectically combine old opportunist ideas with the "latest" bourgeois theories. The Right wing of Social-Democracy has completely broken with Marxism and contraposed so-called democratic socialism to scientific socialism. Its adherents deny the existence of antagonistic classes and the class struggle in bourgeois society; they forcefully deny the necessity of the proletarian revolution and oppose the abolition of the private ownership of the means of production. They assert that capitalism is being "transformed" into socialism.

The Right-wing Socialists began by advocating social reforms in place of the socialist revolution and went as far as to defend state monopoly capitalism. In the past they impressed on the minds of the proletariat that their differences with revolutionary Marxism bore not so much on the ultimate goal of the working-class movement as on the ways of achieving it. Now they openly renounce socialism. Formerly the Right-wing Socialists refused to recognize the class struggle to the point of recognizing the dictatorship of the proletariat. Today they deny, not only the existence of the class struggle in bourgeois society, but also the very existence of antagonistic classes.

Historical experience has shown the bankruptcy of both the ideology and the policy of Social-Democracy. Even when reformist parties come to power they limit themselves to partial reforms that do not affect the rule of the monopoly bourgeoisie. Anti-communism has brought social reformism to an ideological and political impasse. This is one of the main reasons for the crisis of Social-Democracy.

Marxism-Leninism is winning more and more victories. It is winning them because it expresses the vital interests of the working class, of the vast majority of mankind, which seeks peace, freedom, and progress, and because it expresses the ideology of the new society succeeding capitalism.

VIII. Peaceful Coexistence and the Struggle for World Peace

The CPSU considers that the chief aim of its foreign policy activity is to provide peaceful conditions for the building of a communist society of the USSR and developing the world socialist system, and together with the other peace-loving peoples to deliver mankind from a world war of extermination.

The CPSU maintains that forces capable of preserving and promoting universal peace have arisen and are growing in the world. Possibilities are arising for essentially new relations between states.

Imperialism knows no relations between states other than those of domination and subordination, of oppression of the weak by the strong. It bases international relations on diktat and intimidation, on violence and arbitrary rule. It regards wars of aggression as a natural means of settling international issues. For the imperialist countries diplomacy has been, and remains, a tool for imposing their will upon other nations and preparing wars. At the time of the undivided rule of imperialism the issue of war and peace was settled by the finance and industrial oligarchy in utmost secrecy from the peoples.

Socialism confronts imperialism with *a new type of international relations*. The foreign policy of the socialist countries, which is based on the principles of peace, the equality and self-determination of nations, and respect for the independence and sovereignty of all countries, as well as fair, humane methods of socialist diplomacy, are exerting a growing influence on the world situation. At a time when imperialism no longer plays a dominant role in international relations, while the socialist system is playing an increasing role, and when the influence of the countries that have won national independence and of the masses of the people in the capitalist countries has grown very considerably, it is becoming possible for the new principles advanced by socialism to gain the upper hand over the principles of aggressive imperialist policy.

For the first time in history, a situation has arisen in which not only the big states, but also the small ones, the countries which have chosen independent development, and all the states which want peace, are in a position, irrespective of their strength, to pursue an independent foreign policy.

The issue of war and peace is the principal issue of today. Imperialism is the only source of the war danger. The imperialist camp is making preparations for the most terrible crime against mankind—a world thermonuclear war that can bring unprecedented destruction to entire countries and wipe out entire nations. The problem of war and peace has become a life-and-death problem for hundreds of millions of people.

The peoples must concentrate their efforts on curbing the imperialists in good time and preventing them from making use of lethal weapons. *The main thing is to ward off a thermonuclear war, to prevent it from breaking out.* This can be done by the present generation.

The consolidation of the Soviet state and the formation of the world socialist system were historic steps towards the realization of mankind's age-old dream of banishing wars from the life of society. In the socialist part of the world there are no classes or social groups interested in starting a war. Socialism, outstripping capitalism in a number of important branches of science and technology, has supplied the peace-loving peoples with powerful material means of curbing imperialist aggression. Capitalism established its rule with fire and sword, but socialism does not require war to spread its ideals. Its weapon is its superiority over the old system in social organization, political system, economy, the improvement of the standard of living, and spiritual culture.

The socialist system is a natural center of attraction for the peace-loving forces of the globe. The principles of its foreign policy are gaining ever-greater international recognition and support. A vast *peace zone* has taken shape on earth. In addition to the socialist countries, it includes a large group of non-socialist countries that for various reasons are not interested in starting a war. The emergence of those countries in the arena of world politics has substantially altered the balance of forces in favor of peace.

There are a growing number of countries that adhere to a policy of neutrality and strive to safeguard themselves against the hazards of participation in aggressive military blocs.

In the new historical epoch the masses have a far greater opportunity of actively intervening in the settlement of international issues. The peoples are taking the solution of the problem of war and peace into their own hands more and more vigorously. The anti-war movement of the masses, which takes various forms, is a major factor in the struggle for peace. The international working class, the most uncompromising and most consistent fighter against imperialist war, is the great organizing force in this struggle of the people as a whole.

It is possible to avert a world war by the combined efforts of the mighty socialist camp, the peace-loving non-socialist countries, the international working class, and all the forces championing peace. The growing superiority of the socialist forces over the forces of imperialism, of the forces of peace over those of war, will make it actually possible to banish world war from the life of society even before the complete victory of socialism on earth, with capitalism surviving in a part of the world. The victory of socialism throughout the world will do away completely with the social and national causes of all wars. *To abolish war and establish everlasting peace on earth is a historic mission of communism.*

General and complete disarmament under strict international control is a radical way of guaranteeing a durable peace. Imperialism has imposed an unprecedented burden of armaments on the peoples. Socialism sees its duty towards mankind in delivering it from this absurd waste of national wealth. The solution of this problem would have historical significance for mankind. By an active and determined effort the peoples can and must force the imperialists into disarmament.

Socialism has offered mankind the only reasonable principle of maintaining relations between states at a time when the world is divided into two systems—the principle of the peaceful coexistence of states with different social systems, put forward by Lenin.

Peaceful coexistence of the socialist and capitalist countries is an *objective necessity* for the development of human society. *War cannot and must not serve as a means of settling international disputes.* Peaceful coexistence or disastrous war—such are the alternatives offered by history. Should the imperialist aggressors, nevertheless, venture to start a new world war, the peoples will no longer tolerate a system which drags them into devastating wars. They will sweep imperialism away and bury it.

Peaceful coexistence implies renunciation of war as a means of settling international disputes, and their solution by negotiation; equality, mutual understanding and trust between countries; consideration for each other's interests; non-interference in internal affairs; recognition of the right of every people to solve all the problems of their country by themselves; strict respect for the sovereignty and territorial integrity of all countries; promotion of economic and cultural cooperation on the basis of complete equality and mutual benefit.

Peaceful coexistence serves as a basis for the peaceful competition between socialism and capitalism on an international scale and constitutes a specific form of class struggle between them. As they consistently pursue the policy of peaceful coexistence, the socialist countries are steadily strengthening the positions of the world socialist system in its competition with capitalism. Peaceful coexistence affords more favorable opportunities for the struggle of the working class in the capitalist countries and facilitates the struggle of the peoples of the colonial and dependent countries for their liberation. Support for the principle of peaceful coexistence is also in keeping with the interests of that section of the bourgeoisie which realizes that a thermonuclear war would not spare the ruling classes of capitalist society either. The policy of peaceful coexistence is in accord with the vital interests of all mankind, except the big monopoly magnates and the militarists.

The Soviet Union has consistently pursued, and will continue to pursue, the policy of the peaceful coexistence of states with different social systems.

The Communist Party of the Soviet Union advances the following *tasks in the field of international relations:*

To use, together with the other socialist countries, peaceful states and peoples, every means of preventing world war and providing conditions for the complete banishment of war from the life of society.

To pursue a policy of establishing sound international relations, and work for the disbandment of all military blocs opposing each other, the discontinuance of the "cold war" and the propaganda of enmity and hatred among the nations, and the abolition of all air, naval, rocket, and other military bases on foreign territory.

To work for general and complete disarmament under strict international control.

To strengthen relations of fraternal friendship and close cooperation with the countries of Asia, Africa, and Latin America which are fighting to attain or consolidate national independence, with all peoples and states that advocate the preservation of peace.

To pursue an active and consistent policy of improving and developing relations with all capitalist countries, including the United States of America, Great Britain, France, the Federal Republic of Germany, Japan, and Italy, with a view to safeguarding peace.

To contribute in every way to the militant solidarity of all contingents and organizations of the international working class, which oppose the imperialist policy of war.

Steadfastly to pursue a policy of consolidating all the forces fighting against war. All organizations and parties that strive to avert war, the neutralist and pacifist movements and the bourgeois circles that advocate peace and normal relations between countries will meet with understanding and support on the part of the Soviet Union.

To pursue a policy of developing international cooperation in the fields of trade, cultural relations, science, and technology.

To be highly vigilant with regard to the aggressive circles, which are intent on violating peace; to expose, in good time, the initiators of military adventures; to take all necessary steps to safeguard the security and inviolability of our socialist country and the socialist camp as a whole.

The CPSU and the Soviet people as a whole will continue to oppose all wars of conquest, including wars between capitalist countries, and local wars aimed at strangling people's emancipation movements, and consider it their duty to support the sacred struggle of the oppressed peoples and their just anti-imperialist wars of liberation.

The Communist Party of the Soviet Union will hold high the banner of peace and friendship among the nations.

Part Two

THE TASKS OF THE COMMUNIST PARTY OF
THE SOVIET UNION IN BUILDING
A COMMUNIST SOCIETY

Communism—the Bright Future of All Mankind

The building of a communist society has become an immediate practical task for the Soviet people. The gradual development of socialism into communism is an objective law; it has been prepared by the development of Soviet socialist society throughout the preceding period.

What is communism?

Communism is a classless social system with one form of public ownership of the means of production and full social equality of all members of society; under it, the all-round development of people will be accompanied by the growth of the productive forces through continuous progress in science and technology; all the springs of cooperative wealth will flow more abundantly, and the great principle "From each according to his ability, to each according to his needs" will be implemented. Communism is a highly organized society of free, socially conscious working people in which public self-government will be established, a society in which labor for the good of society will become the prime vital requirement of everyone, a necessity recognized by one and all, and the ability of each person will be employed to the greatest benefit of the people.

A high degree of communist consciousness, industry, discipline, and devotion to the public interest are qualities typifying the man of communist society.

Communism ensures the continuous development of social production and rising labor productivity through rapid scientific and technological progress; it equips man with the best and most powerful machines, greatly increases his power over nature and enables him to control its elemental forces to an ever greater extent. The social economy reaches the highest stage of planned organization, and the most effective and rational use is made of the material wealth and labor reserves to meet the growing requirements of the members of society.

Under communism there will be no classes, and the socio-economic and cultural distinctions, and differences in living conditions, between town and countryside will disappear; the countryside will rise to the level of the town in the development of the productive forces and the nature of work, the forms of production relations, living conditions, and the well-being of the population. With the victory of communism mental and physical labor will merge organically in the production activity of people. The intelligentsia will no longer be a distinct social stratum. Workers by hand will have risen in cultural and technological standards to the level of workers by brain.

Thus, communism will put an end to the division of society into classes and social strata, whereas the whole history of mankind, with the exception of its primitive period, was one of class society. Division into opposing classes led to the exploitation of man by man, class struggle, and antagonisms between nations and states.

Under communism all people will have equal status in society, will stand in the same relation to the means of production, will enjoy equal conditions of work and distribution, and will actively participate in the management of public affairs. Harmonious relations will be established between the individual and society on the basis of the unity of public and personal interests. For all their diversity, the requirements of people will express the sound, reasonable requirements of the fully developed person.

The purpose of communist production is to ensure uninterrupted progress of society and to provide all its members with material and cultural benefits according to their growing needs, their individual requirements and tastes. People's requirements will be satisfied from public sources. Articles of personal use will be in the full ownership of each member of society and will be at his disposal.

Communist society, which is based on highly organized production and advanced technology, alters the character of work, but it does not release the members of society from work. It will by no means be a society of anarchy, idleness and inactivity. Every able-bodied person will participate in social labor and thereby ensure the steady growth of the material and spiritual wealth of society. Thanks to the changed character of labor, its better technical equipment, and the high degree of consciousness of all members of society, the latter will work willingly for the public benefit according to their own inclinations.

Communist production demands high standards of organization, precision and discipline, which are ensured, not by compulsion, but through an understanding of public duty, and are determined by the whole pattern of life in communist society. Labor and discipline will not be a burden to people; labor will no longer be a mere source of livelihood—it will be a genuinely creative process and a source of joy.

Communism represents the highest form of organization of public life. All production units and self-governing associations will be harmoniously united in a common planned economy and a uniform rhythm of social labor.

Under communism the nations will draw closer and closer together in all spheres on the basis of a complete identity of economic, political, and spiritual interests, of fraternal friendship and cooperation.

Communism is the system under which the abilities and talents of free man, his best moral qualities, blossom forth and reveal themselves in full. Family relations will be freed once and for all from material considerations and will be based solely on mutual love and friendship.

In defining the basic tasks to be accomplished in building a communist society, the Party is guided by Lenin's great formula: *"Communism is Soviet power plus the electrification of the whole country."*

The CPSU being a party of scientific communism, proposes and fulfils the tasks of communist construction in step with the preparation and maturing of the material and spiritual prerequisites, considering that it would be wrong to jump over necessary stages of development, and that it would be equally wrong to halt at an achieved level and thus check progress. The building of communism must be carried out by successive stages.

In the current decade (1961–70) the Soviet Union, in creating the material and technical basis of communism, will surpass the strongest and richest capitalist country, the United States, in production per head of population; the people's standard of living and their cultural and technical standards will improve substantially; everyone will live in easy circumstances; all collective and state farms will become highly productive and profitable enterprises; the demands of Soviet people for well-appointed housing will, in the main, be satisfied; hard physical work will disappear; the USSR will have the shortest working day.

The material and technical basis of communism will be built up by the *end of the second decade* (1971–80), ensuring an abundance of material and cultural values for the whole population; Soviet society will come close to a stage where it can introduce the principle of distribution according to needs, and there will be a gradual transition to one form of ownership—public ownership. Thus, *a communist society will in the main be built in the USSR*. The construction of communist society will be fully completed in the subsequent period.

The majestic edifice of communism is being erected by the persevering effort of the Soviet people—the working class, the peasantry, and the intelligentsia. The more successful their work, the closer the great goal—communist society.

I. The Tasks of the Party in the Economic Field and in the Creation and Promotion of the Material and Technical Basis of Communism

The main economic task of the Party and the Soviet people is to create *the material and technical basis of communism* within two decades. This means complete electrification of the country and perfection on this basis of the techniques, technologies, and organization of social production in all the fields of the national economy; comprehensive mechanization of production operations and a growing degree of their automation; widespread use of chemistry in the national economy; vigorous development of new, economically effective branches of production, new types of power and new materials; all-round and rational utilization of natural, material, and labor resources; organic fusion of science and production, and rapid scientific and technical progress; a high cultural and technical level for the working people; and substantial superiority over the more developed capitalist countries in productivity of labor, which constitutes the most important prerequisite for the victory of the communist system.

As a result, the USSR will possess productive forces of unparalleled might; it will surpass the technical level of the most developed countries and occupy first place in the world in per capita production. This will serve as a basis for the gradual transformation of socialist social relations into communist relations and for a development of production that will make it possible to meet in abundance the requirements of society and all its members.

In contrast to capitalism, the planned socialist system of economy combines accelerated technical progress with the full employment of all able-bodied citizens. Automation and comprehensive mechanization serve as a material basis for the gradual development of socialist labor into communist labor. Technical progress will require higher standards of production and a higher level of the vocational and general education of all working people. The new machinery will be used to improve radically the Soviet people's working conditions, and make them much easier, to reduce the length of the working day, to improve living conditions, eliminate hard physical work and, subsequently, all unskilled labor.

The material and technical basis will develop and improve continuously together with the evolution of society towards the complete triumph of communism. The level of development of science and technology, and the degree of mechanization and automation of production operations, will steadily rise.

The creation of the material and technical basis of communism will call for huge investments. The task is to utilize these investments most rationally and economically, with the maximum effect and gain of time.

1. THE DEVELOPMENT OF INDUSTRY, BUILDING, TRANSPORT
AND THEIR ROLE IN CREATING THE PRODUCTIVE
FORCES OF COMMUNISM

The creation of material and technical basis of communism, the task of making Soviet industry technologically the best and strongest in the world call for the further development of heavy industry. On this basis, all the other branches of the national economy—agriculture, the consumer goods industries, the building industry, transport and communications, as well as the branches directly concerned with services for the population—trade, public catering, health, housing, and communal services—will be technically reequipped.

A first-class heavy industry, the basis for the country's technical progress and economic might, has been built up in the Soviet Union. The CPSU will continue to devote unflagging attention to the growth of heavy industry and its technical progress. The main task of heavy industry is to meet all the needs of the country's defense and to ensure the development of industries producing consumer goods, so as to satisfy better and in full the requirements of the people, the vital demands of the Soviet man, and to effect the development of the country's productive forces.

With these aims in view, the CPSU plans the following increases in *total industrial output:*

Within the current 10 years, approximately 150 per cent, exceeding the level of U.S. industrial output.

Within 20 years, by not less than 500 per cent, leaving the present overall volume of U.S. industrial output far behind.

To achieve this, it is necessary to raise the *productivity of labor* in industry by more than 100 per cent within 10 years, and by 300–350 per cent within 20 years. In 20 years' time labor productivity in Soviet industry will exceed the present level of labor productivity in the United States by roughly 100 per cent, and considerably more in terms of per-hour output, due to the reduction of the working day in the USSR.

Such an intensive development of industry will call for major progressive changes in its *structure.* The role of new branches ensuring the greatest technical progress will grow very considerably. The less effective fuels, types of power, raw and semi-manufactured materials will be increasingly superseded by highly effective ones, and their comprehensive use will increase greatly. The share of synthetic materials, metals, and alloys with new properties will increase considerably. New types of automatic and electronic machinery, instruments, and apparatus will be rapidly introduced on a large scale.

Electrification, which is the pivot of the economic construction of communist society, plays a key role in the development of all economic branches and in the effecting of all modern technological progress. It is therefore important to ensure the priority development of *electric power* output. The plan for the electrification of the country provides for an almost threefold increase in the power capacity per industrial worker within the present decade; a considerable expansion of industries with a high rate of power consumption through the supply of cheap power; and extensive electrification of transport, agriculture, and the household in town and countryside. The electrification of the country will on the whole be completed in the course of the second decade.

The annual output of electricity must be brought up to about 900,000–1,000,000 million kwh by the end of the first decade, and to 2,700,000–3,000,000 million kwh by the end of the second decade. For this it will be necessary in the course of 20 years to increase accordingly the installed capacities of electric power plants and to build hundreds of thousands of kilometers of high-tension transmission and distribution lines throughout the country. A single power grid for the whole USSR will be built and will have sufficient capacity reserves to transmit electric power from the eastern regions to the European part of the country; it will link up with the power grids of other socialist countries.

As atomic energy becomes cheaper, the construction of atomic power stations will be expanded, especially in areas poor in other power sources, and the use of atomic energy for peaceful purposes in the national economy, in medicine and science will increase.

The further rapid expansion of the output of *metals and fuels*, the basis of modern industry, remains one of the major economic tasks. Within 20 years, metallurgy will develop sufficiently to produce about 250 million tons of steel a year. Steel output must cover fully the requirements of the national economy in accordance with the technological progress achieved in that period. The output of light, non-ferrous, and rare metals will grow appreciably; the output of aluminum and its use in electrification, engineering, building, and the household will increase considerably. A steady effort will be made to ensure priority development of oil and gas production as these items will be used increasingly as raw materials for the chemical industry. Coal, gas, and oil extraction must meet the requirements of the national economy in full. The most progressive and economic methods of extracting mineral fuels are to be applied extensively.

One of the most important tasks is the all-round development of the *chemical* industry, and the full use in all economic fields of the achievements of modern chemistry. This provides greater opportunities to increase the national wealth and the output of new, better, and cheaper capital and consumer goods. Metal, wood, and other materials will be increasingly replaced by economical, durable, light synthetic materials. The output of mineral fertilizers and chemical weed and pest killers will rise sharply.

Of primary importance for the technical reequipment of the entire national economy is the development of *mechanical engineering*, with special stress laid on the accelerated production of automated production lines and machines, automatic, tele-mechanic, and electronic devices and precision instruments. The designing of highly efficient machines consuming less raw materials and power, and leading to higher productivity of labor will make rapid progress. The requirements of the national economy in all types of modern machines, machine tools, and apparatus, as well as spare parts and instruments will be met in full.

The development of mechanical engineering in the first decade will serve as the basis for *comprehensive mechanization* in industry, agriculture, building, transport, and in the municipal economy. Comprehensive mechanization will exclude manual loading and unloading jobs and strenuous labor in both the basic and auxiliary operations.

In the 20 years comprehensive *automation* will be effected on a mass scale, with increasing emphasis on fully automated shops and factories, making for high technical and economic efficiency. Introduction of the very latest systems of automated control will be speeded up. Cybernetics, electronic computer and control systems will be widely applied in production processes in industry, building, and transport, in scientific research, planning, designing, accounting, statistics, and management.

The vast scope of capital construction calls for the rapid

development and technological modernization of the *building and building materials industry* up to a level meeting the requirements of the national economy, for a maximum reduction of building schedules and costs, and an improvement of the quality of building through its continuous industrialization; it is essential to go over completely at the earliest possible time to erecting wholly prefabricated buildings and structures of standard design made of large prefabricated elements.

The CPSU will concentrate its efforts on ensuring a rapid increase in the output of *consumer goods*. The growing resources of industry must be used more and more to meet fully all the requirements of Soviet people and to build and equip enterprises and establishments catering to the household and cultural needs of the population. Along with the accelerated development of all branches of the light and food industries, the share of consumer goods in the output of heavy industry will also increase. More electricity and gas will be supplied to the population.

The growth of the national economy will call for the accelerated development of *all transport facilities*. The most important tasks in the sphere of transport are: expansion of transport and road construction to meet in full the requirements of the national economy and the population in all modes of transport; further modernization of the railways and other transport systems; a considerable increase of the speed of rail, sea, and river traffic; the coordinated development of all types of transport as components of a single transport network. The share of pipe transport will increase.

A single deep-water system will link the main inland waterways of the European part of the USSR.

A ramified network of modern roads will be built throughout the country. The automobile fleet will increase sufficiently to meet fully freight and passenger requirements; car hire centers will be organized on a large scale. Air transport will become a means of mass passenger traffic extending to all parts of the country.

Up-to-date *jet* engineering will develop rapidly, above all in air transport, as well as in space exploration.

All means of *communication* (post, radio, and television, telephone and telegraph) will be developed still more. All regions of the country will have reliable communications and a link-up system of television stations.

Full-scale communist construction calls for a more rational *geographic distribution* of the industries in order to save social labor and ensure the comprehensive development of areas and the specialization of their industries, do away with the over-population of big cities, faciliate the elimination of essential distinctions between town and countryside, and further even out the economic levels of different parts of the country.

To gain time, priority will be given to developing easily exploited natural resources that provide the greatest economic effect.

Industry in the areas to the *east of the Urals,* where there are immense natural riches, raw material, and power resources, will expand greatly.

The following must be achieved within the next 20 years: in Siberia and Kazakhstan—the creation of new power bases using deposits of cheap coal or the water-power resources of the Angara and Yenisei rivers; the organization of big centers of power-consuming industries, the development of new rich ore, oil, and coal deposits; and the construction of a number of new large machine-building centers; in areas along the Volga, in the Urals, North Caucasus, and Central Asia—the rapid development of the power, oil, gas, and chemical industries and the development of ore deposits. Alongside the development of the existing old metallurgical centers in the Urals and the Ukraine, the completion is envisaged of the country's third metallurgical base in Siberia, and the building of two new ones; in the central European part of the USSR, utilizing the iron ore of the Kursk iron fields, and in Kazakhstan. Soviet people will be able to carry out daring plans to change the courses of some northern rivers and regulate their discharge for the purpose of utilizing vast water resources for the irrigation and watering of arid areas.

The economy in the European part of the USSR which contains the bulk of the population and where there are great opportunities for increased industrial output, will make further substantial progress.

The maximum acceleration of scientific and engineering prog-

ress is a major national task which calls for daily effort to reduce the time spent on designing new machinery and introducing it in industry. It is necessary to promote in every way the initiative of economic councils, enterprises, social organizations, scientists, engineers, designers, workers, and collective farmers in creating and applying new technical improvements. Of utmost importance is the material and moral stimulation of mass invention and rationalization movements, of enterprises, shops, state and collective farms, teams, and innovators who master the production of new machinery and utilize it skillfully.

The Party will do everything to *enhance the role of science* in the building of communist society; it will encourage research to discover new possibilities for the development of the productive forces, and the rapid and extensive application of the latest scientific and technical achievements; a decisive advancement in experimental work, including research directly at enterprises, and the efficient organization of scientific and technical information and of the whole system of studying and disseminating progressive Soviet and foreign methods. Science will itself in full measure become a direct productive force.

The constant *improvement in the technology* of all industries and production branches is a requisite for their development. Technological progress will make man's labor easier, facilitate substantial intensification and accleration of production and give it the highest degree of precision, will facilitate the standardization of mass production items and maximum use of production lines. Machining will be supplemented and, when necessary, replaced by chemical methods, the technological use of electricity, electrochemistry, etc.; radio-electronics, semiconductors and ultra-sound will occupy a more and more important place in production techniques. The construction of new, technically up-to-date enterprises will proceed side by side with the reconstruction of those now in existence and the replacement and modernization of their equipment.

The development of the *specialization and cooperation, and appropriate combination of related enterprises* is a most important condition for technical progress and the rational organization of social labor. Articles of similar type should be manufactured mainly at large specialized plants, with provision for their most rational geographic distribution.

New techniques and the reduction of the working day calls for *a higher level in the organization of work*. Technical progress and better organization must be fully utilized to increase labor productivity and reduce production costs at every enterprise. This implies a higher rate of increase in labor productivity as compared with the rate of growth of wages, better rate-fixing, prevention of loss of working time, and operation on a profitable basis in all sectors of production.

Most important will be systematic improvement of the qualifications of those working in industry and other branches of the economy in connection with technical progress. The planned training, instruction, and rational employment of those released from various jobs and transferred to other jobs due to mechanization and automation are essential.

Existing enterprises will be improved and developed into enterprises of communist society. Typical of this process will be new machinery, high standards of production organization and efficiency through increased automation of production operations and the introduction of automation into control; an improvement of the cultural and technical standards of the workers, the increasing fusion of physical and mental labor and the growing proportion of engineers and technicians in every industrial enterprise; the expansion of research, and closer links between enterprises and research institutes; promotion of the emulation movement, the application of the achievements of science and the best forms of labor organization and best methods of raising labor productivity, the extensive participation of workers' collectives in the management of enterprises, and the spreading of communist forms of labor.

2. THE DEVELOPMENT OF AGRICULTURE AND SOCIAL RELATIONS IN THE COUNTRYSIDE

Along with a powerful industry, a flourishing, versatile and highly productive agriculture is an imperative condition for the building of communism. The Party organizes a great development of productive forces in agriculture, which will make it possible to accomplish two basic, closely related tasks: (a) to build up an abundance of high-quality food products for the population and of raw materials for industry, and (b) to effect the gradual transition of social relations in the Soviet countryside to communist relations and eliminate, in the main, the distinctions between town and country.

The chief means of achieving progress in agriculture and satisfying the growing needs of the country in farm produce are comprehensive mechanization and consistent *intensification:* high efficiency of crop farming and stock-breeding based on science and progressive experience in all kolkhozes and state farms, a steep rise in the yield capacity of all crops and greater output per hectare with the minimum outlay of labor and funds. On this basis, it is necessary to achieve an unintermittent growth of agricultural production in keeping with the needs of society. Agriculture will approach the level of industry in technical equipment and the organization of production; farm labor will turn into a variety of industrial labor, and the dependence of agriculture upon the elements will decrease considerably, and ultimately drop to a minimum.

The development of virgin and unused land and establishment of new large-scale state farms, the reorganization of the machine and tractor stations, the sale of implements of production to the collective farms, introduction of new planning procedures, and the enhancement of material incentives for agricultural workers—all constituted an important stage in the development of agriculture. The Party will continue to devote considerable attention to the development of agriculture in the virgin and unused land development areas.

The further advance of the countryside to communism will proceed through the development and improvement of the two forms of socialist farming—the kolkhozes and state farms.

The *kolkhoz system* is an integral part of Soviet socialist society. It is a way charted by V. I. Lenin for the gradual transition of the peasantry to communism; it has stood the test of history and conforms to the distinctive features of the peasantry.

Kolkhoz farming accords in full with the level and needs of the development of modern productive forces in the countryside, and makes possible effective use of new machinery and the achievements of science, and rational employment of manpower. The kolkhoz blends the personal interests of the peasants with common, nation-wide interests, individual with collective interest in the results of production, and offers extensive opportunities for raising the incomes and the well-being of peasants on the basis of growing labor productivity. It is essential to make the most of the possibilities and advantages of the kolkhoz system. By virtue of the social form of its economy—its organizational structure and its democratic groundwork—which will develop more and more, the kolkhoz ensures that production is run by the kolkhoz members themselves, that their creative initiative is enhanced, and that the collective farmers are educated in the communist spirit. The kolkhoz is a school of communism for the peasantry.

Economic advancement of the kolkhoz system creates conditions for the gradual *rapprochement* and, in the long run, also for the merging of kolkhoz property and the property of the whole people into one communist property.

The *state farms,* which are the leading socialist agricultural enterprises, play an ever-increasing role in the development of agriculture. The state farms must serve the kolkhozes as a model of progressive, scientifically-managed, economically profitable social production, of high efficiency and labor productivity.

The CPSU proceeds from the fact that the further consolidation of the *unbreakable alliance of the working class and the kolkhoz peasantry* is of crucial political and socio-economic importance for the building of communism in the USSR.

A. *Building up an abundance of agricultural produce.*

In order fully to satisfy the requirements of the entire population and of the national economy in agricultural produce, the task is to increase the *aggregate volume of agricultural production* in 10 years by about 150 per cent, and in 20 years by 250 per cent. Agricultural output must keep ahead of the growing demand. In the first decade the Soviet Union will outstrip the

United States in output of the key agricultural products per head of population.

Accelerated growth of *grain* production is the chief link in the further development of all agriculture and a basis for the rapid growth of stock-breeding. The aggregate grain crops will more than double in twenty years, and their yield capacity will double. The output of wheat, maize, cereal, and leguminous crops will increase substantially.

Livestock breeding will develop at a rapid rate. The output of animal products will rise: meat about threefold in the first ten years and nearly fourfold in twenty years, and milk more than double in the first decade and nearly threefold in twenty years. The planned increase in the output of animal products will be achieved by increasing the cattle and poultry population, improving stock and productivity, and building up reliable fodder resources, chiefly maize, sugar-beet, fodder beans, and other crops.

Productivity of labor in agriculture will rise not less than 150 per cent in ten years, and five- to sixfold in twenty years. The rapid rise of the productivity of farm labor—at a higher rate than in industry—will serve to eliminate the lag of agriculture behind industry and will turn it into a highly developed branch of the economy of communist society.

The further mechanization of agriculture, introduction of *comprehensive mechanization* and use of automatic devices and highly efficient and economical machinery adapted to the conditions of each zone will be the basis for the growth of productivity of farm labor.

The Party considers rapid *electrification* of agriculture one of the most important tasks. All state farms and kolkhozes will be supplied electric power for production and domestic purposes, from the state power grid and from power stations to be built in the countryside.

The technical reequipment of agriculture must combine with the most progressive forms and methods of the organization of labor and production and the maximum improvement of the cultural and technical education of farm workers. There will be increasingly more qualified workers with special agricultural

training and proficient in the use of new machinery in the kolkhozes and state farms. Good care and maintenance of agricultural machinery and its highly efficient use are extremely important.

To ensure high, stable, steadily increasing harvests, to deliver
agriculture from the baneful effects of the elements, especially
droughts, steeply to raise land fertility, and rapidly to advance
livestock breeding, it is necessary:

To effect a scientifically expedient distribution of agriculture
by natural-economic zones and districts, and a more thorough
and stable *specialization* of agriculture with priority given to
the type of farm product where the best conditions for it exist
and the greatest saving in outlay is achieved.

To introduce on all collective and state farms a *scientifically
motivated system of land cultivation and animal husbandry* consistent with local conditions and with the specialization of each
farm, ensuring the most effective use of the land and the most
economically expedient combination of branches, the best structure of crop acreage with the substitution of high-yield and
valuable crops for crops of little value and those giving low
yields; to ensure that every kolkhoz and state farm masters the
most advanced methods of crop farming with the application of
efficient crop rotation and sow high-grade seed only; to build
up reliable fodder resources in all districts and to introduce the
foremost stock-breeding techniques in kolkhozes and state farms.

To effect a rational *introduction of chemicals* in all branches
of agriculture, to meet all its needs in mineral fertilizers and
chemical and biological means of combating weeds, blights, diseases, and plant and animal pests, and to ensure the best use of
local fertilizers in all collective and state farms.

To apply broadly biological achievements, and especially mi-
crobiology, which is assuming ever greater importance for the
improvement of soil fertility.

To carry through a far-flung *irrigation program:* to irrigate
and water millions of hectares of new land in the arid areas and
improve existing irrigated farming; to expand field-protective
afforestation, building of water reservoirs, watering of pastures
and melioration of overmoist land; and to combat systematically

the water and wind erosion of soil. Considerable attention will be devoted to the conservation and rational use of forests, water reservoirs, and other natural resources, and to their restocking and development.

The Party will promote the development of *agricultural science,* focus the creative efforts of scientists on the key problems of agricultural progress, and work for the practical application and extensive introduction of the achievements of science and progressive production experience in crop farming and stockbreeding. Research institutions and experimental stations are to become important links in agricultural management, and scientists and specialists must become the direct organizers of farm production. Each region or group of regions of the same zonal type should have agricultural research centers, with their own large-scale farms and up-to-date material and technical resources, to work out recommendations for collective and state farms applicable to the given district. Agricultural research and educational establishments and institutions must be chiefly located in rural areas and be directly associated with farm production, so that students may learn while working and work while learning.

B. *Kolkhozes and state farms on the road to communism;*
remolding social relations in the countryside.

The economic basis for the development of kolkhozes and state farms lies in the continuous growth and best use of their productive forces, improvement of the organization of production and methods of management, steady rise of labor productivity and strict observance of the principle: higher payment for good work, for better results. On this basis the kolkhozes and state farms will become to an increasing degree enterprises of the communist type in production relations, character of labor, and the living and cultural standards of their personnel.

The policy of the Party in relation to the kolkhozes is based on blending country-wide interests with the material interest of the kolkhozes and their members in the results of their labor. The state will promote the growth of the productive forces of the kolkhoz system and the economic advancement of all kolkhozes; concurrently, the kolkhoz peasantry must contribute more widely to the building of communist society.

The state will ensure the full satisfaction of the needs of the kolkhozes in modern machinery, spare parts, chemicals, and other means of production, will train new hundreds of thousands of skilled farm workers, and will considerably increase capital investments in the countryside, in addition to the greater investments which the collective farms will themselves make. The amount of manufactured goods made available to the countryside will increase greatly.

Strict observance of their contracted commitments to the state by the kolkhozes and their members is an inviolable principle of their participation in the development of the national economy.

The system of state purchasing must aim at increasing the amount and improving the quality of the agricultural products bought, on the basis of an all-round advancement of kolkhoz farming. It is essential to coordinate the planning of state purchases and the production plans of the kolkhozes, with utmost consideration for the interests of agricultural production, its proper distribution and specialization.

The policy in the sphere of state purchasing prices of agricultural produce and state selling prices of means of production for the countryside must take account of the interests of extended reproduction in both industry and agriculture and of the need to accumulate funds in the kolkhozes. It is essential that the level of state purchasing prices encourage the kolkhozes to raise labor productivity and reduce production expenses, since greater farm output and lower production costs are the basis of greater incomes for the kolkhozes.

The proper ratio of *accumulation and consumption* in the distribution of incomes is a prerequisite of successful kolkhoz development. The kolkhozes cannot develop without continuously extending their commonly-owned assets for production, insurance, cultural and community needs. At the same time, it must be a standing rule for every kolkhoz to raise its members' incomes from collective farming and to enhance their living standard as labor productivity rises.

Great importance attaches to improved methods of rate-setting and labor remuneration at kolkhozes, supplementary remuneration of labor, and other incentives to obtain better production results. Increasingly equal economic conditions must be provided to improve the incomes of kolkhozes existing under unequal natural-economic conditions in different zones, and also within the zones, in order to put into effect more consistently the principle of equal pay for equal work on a scale embracing the entire kolkhoz system. Farming on all collective farms must be based on the principle of profitability.

In its organizational work and economic policy, the Party will strive to overcome the lag of the economically weak kolkhozes and to turn all kolkhozes into economically strong, high-income farms in the course of the next few years. The Party sets the task of continuously improving and educating kolkhoz personnel, of ensuring the further extension of kolkhoz democracy, and promoting the principle of collectivism in management.

As the kolkhozes develop, their basic production facilities will expand, and modern technical means will become dominant.

The economic advancement of the kolkhozes will make it possible to perfect *kolkhoz internal relations:* to raise the degree to which production is socialized; to bring the rate-setting, organization and payment of labor closer to the level and the forms employed at state enterprises and effect a transition to a guaranteed monthly income; to develop community services more broadly (public catering, kindergartens and nurseries, and other services, etc.).

At a certain point the collective production at kolkhozes will achieve a level at which it will satisfy fully members' requirements. On this basis, supplementary individual farming will gradually become economically unnecessary. When collective production at the kolkhozes is able to replace in full production on the supplementary individual plots of the kolkhoz members, when the collective farmers see for themselves that their supplementary individual farming is unprofitable, they will give it up of their own accord.

As the productive forces increase, inter-kolkhoz production ties will develop and the socialization of production will tran-

scend the limits of individual kolkhozes. The building, jointly
by several kolkhozes, of enterprises and cultural and welfare
institutions, state-kolkhoz power stations and enterprises for the
primary processing, storage, and transportation of farm products
for various types of building, the manufacture of building materials and elements, etc., should be encouraged. As the commonly-owned assets increase, the kolkhozes will participate more
and more in establishing enterprises and cultural and welfare
institutions for general public use, boarding schools, clubs, hospitals and holiday homes. All these developments, which must
proceed on a voluntary basis and when the necessary economic
conditions are available, will gradually impart to kolkhoz cooperative property the nature of public property.

The state farms have a long way to travel in their development
—to increase production and improve its quality continuously, to
concentrate on attaining high rates of growth of labor productivity, steadily to reduce production costs and raise farm profitability. This calls for the economically expedient specialization
of state farms. Their role in supplying food to the urban population will grow. They must become mechanized and well-organized
first-class factories of grain, cotton, meat, milk, wool, vegetable,
fruit, and other products, and must develop seed farming and
pure-strain animal hubandry to the utmost.

The material and technical basis of the state farms will be
extended and improved, and the living and cultural conditions
at the state farms will approach those in towns. State-farm management should follow a more and more democratic pattern
which will allot a greater role to the personnel, to general meetings and production conferences, in deciding production, cultural, and other community issues.

As the kolkhozes and state farms develop, their production
ties with each other and with local industrial enterprises will
grow stronger. The practice of jointly organizing various enterprises will expand. This will ensure a fuller and more balanced
use of manpower and production resources throughout the year,
raise the productivity of social labor and enhance the living and
cultural standards of the population. Agrarian-industrial associations will gradually emerge wherever economically expedient,

in which, given appropriate specialization and cooperation of agricultural and industrial enterprises, agriculture will combine organically with the industrial processing of its produce.

As production in collective and state farms develops and social relations within them advance, agriculture rises to a higher level, affording the possibility of transition to communist forms of production and distribution. The kolkhozes will draw level in economic conditions with the nationally-owned agricultural enterprises. They will turn into highly developed mechanized farms. By virtue of high labor productivity all kolkhozes will become economically powerful. Kolkhoz members will be provided for adequately and their requirements fully satisfied out of collective-farm production. They will have the services of catering establishments, bakeries, laundries, kindergartens and nurseries, clubs, libraries, and sports grounds. The payment of labor will be the same as at nationally-owned enterprises; they will enjoy all forms of social security (pensions, holidays, etc.) out of kolkhoz and state funds.

Gradually, the kolkhoz villages will grow into amalgamated urban communities with modern housing facilities, public amenities and services, and cultural and medical institutions. The rural population will ultimately attain the level of the urban population in cultural and living conditions.

Elimination of socio-economic and cultural distinctions between town and country and of differences in their living conditions will be one of the greatest gains of communist construction.

3. MANAGEMENT OF THE NATIONAL ECONOMY AND PLANNING

The building of the material and technical basis of communism calls for a continuous improvement in economic management and planning. Chief emphasis at all levels of planning and economic management must be laid on the most rational and effective use of the material, labor and financial resources and natural wealth and on the elimination of excessive expenditure and of losses. The immutable law of economic development is to achieve in the interests of society the highest results at the lowest cost. In the improvement of economic management utmost stress is to be laid on making the apparatus of management simpler and cheaper to run.

Planning must at all levels concentrate on the rapid development and introduction of new techniques. It is essential that progressive, scientifically substantiated norms for the use of means of production be continuously improved and strictly observed in all sectors of the national economy.

The Party attaches prime importance to more *effective investments,* the choice of the most profitable and economical trends in capital construction, achievement of the maximum growth of output per invested ruble, and reduction of the time lapse between investment and return. It is necessary continuously to improve the structure of capital investments and to expand that portion of them which is spent on equipment, machinery, and machine tools.

It should be an immutable condition of planning and economic organization to concentrate investments in the decisive sectors of industry, to eliminate scattering of allocations and to accelerate the commissioning of projects in construction.

Continuous improvement of the *quality of output* is an imperative requirement of economic development. The quality of goods produced by Soviet enterprises must be considerably higher than that of the best capitalist enterprises. For this purpose, it is necessary to apply a wide range of measures, including public control, and to enhance the role of quality indexes in planning, in the assessment of the work of enterprises, and in socialist emulation.

Communist construction presupposes the maximum development of *democratic principles of management* coupled with a strengthening and improvement of *centralized economic management by the state.* Economic independence and the rights of local organs and enterprises will continue to expand within the framework of the single national economic plan. Plans and recommendations made at lower levels, beginning with enterprises, must play an increasing role in planning.

Centralized planning should concentrate chiefly on working out and ensuring the fulfilment of the key targets of the economic plans with the greatest consideration paid to recommendations made at lower levels; on coordinating and dovetailing plans drawn up locally; on spreading scientific and technical achievements and advanced production experience; on enforcing a single state policy in the spheres of technical progress, capital investment, distribution of industry, payment of labor, prices, and finance, and a unified system of accounting and statistics.

It is essential that the national economy develop on a strictly *proportionate basis,* that economic disproportions are prevented in good time, ensuring sufficient economic reserves as a condition for stable high rates of economic development, uninterrupted operation of enterprises, and continuous improvement of the people's well-being.

The growing scale of the national economy, the rapid development of science and technology call for an improvement of the scientific level of planning, designing, accounting and statistics. A better scientific, technical, and economic substantiation of the plans will ensure their greater stability, which also presupposes timely correction and amendment of plans in the course of their fulfilment. Planning must be continuous, the annual and long-term plans must be organically integrated, and the funds and material and technical resources must be provided for.

Firm and consistent discipline, day-to-day control, and determined elimination of elements of parochialism and of a narrow departmental approach in economic affairs are necessary conditions for successful communist construction.

There must be a further expansion of the role and responsibility of *local bodies* in economic management. The transfer of a number of functions of economic management by the all-Union bodies to those of the republics, by republican bodies to those of the regions, and by regional bodies to those of the districts should be continued. It is necessary to improve the work of the economic councils as the most viable form of management in industry and building conforming to the present level of the productive forces. The improvement of the work of economic councils within the economic administration areas will also be accompanied by greater coordination of the work of the economic bodies, in order better to organize the planned, comprehensive economic development of such major economic areas as the Urals, the Volgaside area, West Siberia, East Siberia, the Far East, Transcaucasia, the Baltic area, Central Asia, etc.

Extension of the operative independence and *initiative of enterprises* on the basis of the state-plan targets is essential in order to mobilize untapped resources and make more effective use of capital investments, production facilities, and finances. It is necessary to enhance the role of enterprises and stimulate their interest in introducing the latest machinery and using production capacities to the utmost.

The selection, training, and promotion of people who directly head enterprises and kolkhozes, who organize and manage production, are of decisive importance in economic management. The sphere of material production is the main sphere in the life of society; the most capable people must, therefore, be given leading posts at enterprises.

The direct and most active participation of *trade unions* in elaborating and realizing economic plans, in matters concerning the labor of factory and office workers, in setting up organs of economic administration and of management of enterprises, must be extended more and more at the big centers and the localities. The role of the collectives of factory and office workers in matters concerning the work of enterprises must be enhanced.

In the process of communist construction economic management will make use of material and moral incentives for high production figures. Proper combination of material and moral labor incentives is a great creative factor in the struggle for communism. In the course of the advance to communism the importance of moral labor incentives, public recognition of achieved results, and the sense of responsibility of each for the common cause will become continuously greater.

The entire system of planning and assessing the work of central and local organizations, enterprises and collective farms must stimulate their interest in higher plan targets and the maximum dissemination of progressive production experience. Initiative and successes in finding and using new ways of improving the quantitative and qualitative indexes of production should be specially encouraged.

There must be a continuous improvement in rate setting, the

system of labor payments and bonuses, in the financial control over the quantity and quality of work, in the elimination of leveling, and the stimulation of collective forms of material incentives raising the interest of each employee in the high efficiency of the enterprise as a whole.

It is necessary in communist construction to make full use of commodity-money relations in keeping with their new content in the socialist period. In this, such instruments of economic development as cost accounting, money, price, production cost, profit, trade, credit, and finance play a big part. With the transition to the single communist form of people's property and the communist system of distribution, commodity-money relations will become economically outdated and will wither away.

The important role of the state budget in distributing the social product and national income will prevail throughout the period of full-scale communist construction. There will be a further strengthening of the monetary and credit system, a consolidation of Soviet currency, a steady rise of the purchasing power of the ruble and an increase in the importance of the ruble in the international arena.

It is necessary to promote profitable operation of enterprises, to work for economy and thrift, reduction of losses, lower production costs, and higher profitability. The price system should be continuously improved in conformity with the tasks of communist construction, technical progress, growth of production and consumption, and the reduction of production expenditures. Prices must, to a growing extent, reflect the socially-necessary outlays of labor, ensure return of production and circulation expenditures, and a certain profit for each normally operating enterprise. Systematic, economically justified price reductions based on growth of labor productivity and reduction of production costs are the main trend of the price policy in the period of communist construction.

Soviet society possesses immense national assets. For this reason, the role of accounting and control over the maintenance and proper use of the national wealth increases. Thrift, the proper use of every ruble belonging to the people, competent expenditure of funds, the continuous improvement of planning and methods of management, improvement of organization and conscious discipline, and development of the initiative of the people are powerful means of accelerating the advance of Soviet society to communism.

II. The Tasks of the Party in Improving the Living Standard of the People

The heroic labor of the Soviet people has produced a powerful and versatile economy. There is now every possibility to improve rapidly the living standard of the entire population—the workers, peasants, and intellectuals. The CPSU sets the historically important task of *achieving in the Soviet Union a living standard higher than that of any of the capitalist countries.*

This task will be effected by: (a) raising individual payment according to the quantity and quality of work done, coupled with reduction of retail prices and abolition of taxes paid by the population; (b) increase of the public consumption fund intended for the satisfaction of the requirements of members of society irrespective of the quantity and quality of their labor, that is, free of charge (education, medical treatment, pensions, maintenance of children at children's institutions, transition to cost-free use of public amenities, etc.).

The rise of the real incomes of the population will be outstripped by a rapid increase in the amount of commodities and services, and by extensive construction of dwellings and cultural and service buildings.

Soviet people will be more prosperous than working people in the developed capitalist countries even if average incomes will be equal, because in the Soviet Union the national income is distributed in the interests of all members of society and there are no parasitical classes as in the bourgeois countries who appropriate and squander immense wealth plundered from millions of working people.

The Party acts upon Lenin's thesis that communist construction must be based upon the principle of material incentive. In the coming twenty years payment according to one's work will remain the principal source for satisfying the material and cultural needs of the working people.

The disparity between high and comparatively low incomes must be steadily reduced. Increasingly greater numbers of unskilled personnel will become skilled, and the diminishing difference in proficiency and labor productivity will be accompanied by a steady reduction of disparities in the level of pay. As the living standard of the entire population rises, low income levels will approach the higher, and the disparity between the incomes of peasants and workers, low-paid and high-paid personnel, and of the populations of different parts of the country, will gradually shrink.

At the same time, as the country advances towards communism, personal needs will be increasingly met out of public consumption funds, whose rate of growth will exceed the rate of growth of payments for labor. The transition to communist distribution will be completed after the principle of distribution according to one's work will outlive itself, that is, when there will be an abundance of material and cultural wealth and labor will become a prime necessity of life for all members of society.

A. *Provision of a high level of income and consumption for the whole population. Expansion of trade.*

The national income of the USSR in the next ten years will increase nearly 150 per cent, and about 400 per cent in twenty years. The real income per head of population will increase by more than 250 per cent in twenty years. In the first decade already the real incomes of all factory, professional and office workers (including public funds) per employed person will, on the average, be almost doubled, and the incomes of the low-paid brackets of factory and office workers will increase approximately threefold. Thus, by the end of the first decade there will be no low-paid brackets of factory and office workers in the country.

By virtue of higher rates of growth of the labor productivity of collective farmers their real incomes will grow more rapidly than the incomes of factory workers, and will, on an average per employed person, more than double in the next ten years and increase more than fourfold in twenty years.

The wages of such numerically large sections of the Soviet intelligentsia as engineers and technicians, agronomists and stock-breeding experts, teachers, medical and cultural workers, will rise considerably.

As the incomes of the population grow, *the general level of popular consumption will rise rapidly*. The entire population will be able adequately to satisfy its need in high-quality and varied foodstuffs. The share of animal products (meat, fats, dairy produce), fruit, and high-grade vegetables in popular consumption will rise substantially in the near future. The demand of all sections of the population for high-quality consumer goods— attractive and durable clothes, footwear and goods improving and adorning the daily life of Soviet people, such as comfortable modern furniture, up-to-date domestic goods, a wide range of goods for cultural purposes, etc.—will be amply satisfied. Production of motor cars will be considerably extended to service the population.

Output of consumer goods must meet the growing consumer demand in full, and must conform to its changes. Timely output of goods in accordance with the varied demand of the population, with consideration for local, national, and climatic conditions, is an imperative requirement for all the consumer industries.

Soviet trade will be further developed as a necessary condition to meeting the growing requirements of the people. Good shopping facilities will be made available throughout the country, and progressive forms of trading will be widely applied. The material and technical basis of Soviet trade—the network of shops, warehouses, refrigerators, and vegetable stores—will be extended.

Consumer cooperatives, which are to improve trade in the countryside and to organize sales of surplus agricultural produce, will develop. Collective-farm trade will lose none of its importance.

An abundance of material and cultural benefits for the whole population will be attained in the course of the second decade, and material prerequisites will be created for the transition in the period to follow to the communist principle of distribution according to need.

B. *Solution of the housing problem and improvement of living conditions.*

The CPSU sets the task of solving the most acute problem in the improvement of the well-being of the Soviet people—the housing problem. In the course of the first decade an end will be put to the housing shortage in the country. Families that are still housed in overcrowded and substandard dwellings, will get new flats. At the end of the second decade, every family, including newlyweds, will have a comfortable flat conforming to the requirements of hygiene and cultural living. Peasant houses of the old type will, in the main, give place to new modern dwellings, or—wherever possible—they will be rebuilt and appropriately improved. In the course of the second decade housing will gradually become rent-free for all citizens.

Town building, architecture and planning aimed at designing modern, comfortable towns and communities, industrial projects, dwellings and public buildings economical to build and to maintain, are acquiring great importance. Towns and communities must constitute a rational and comprehensive organization of industrial zones, residential areas, public and cultural institutions, communal services, transport, engineering equipment and power sources ensuring the best possible conditions for labor, life, and leisure.

An extensive program of public-services construction and of improvements in all towns and workers' estates will be carried out in the coming period, which will involve completion of their electrification, the necessary gasification, provision of telephone communications, public transport facilities, waterworks, sewerage, and measures for the further improvement of sanitary conditions in towns and other populated localities, including tree planting, pond building, and effective measures to combat air, soil and water pollution. Well-appointed small and middle-size towns will be increasingly developed, making for better and healthier living conditions.

Public transport facilities (tramways, buses, trolley-buses, and subways) will become free in the course of the second decade, and at the end of it such public amenities as water, gas, and heating will also be free.

C. *Reduction of working hours and the further improvement of working conditions.*

In the coming ten years the country will go over to *a six-hour working day* with one day off a week, or *a 35-hour working week* with two days off, and on underground jobs and enterprises with harmful working conditions to a five-hour working day or a 30-hour five-day working week.

By virtue of a corresponding rise in labor productivity, transition to a still shorter working week will be begun in the second decade.

The Soviet Union will thus have the world's shortest and, concurrently, the most productive and highest-paid working day. Working people will have much more leisure time, and this will add to their opportunities of improving their cultural and technical level.

The length of the annual paid holidays of working people will be increased together with the reduction of the working day. Gradually the minimum length of leave for all industrial, professional, and office workers will increase to three weeks and subsequently to one month. Paid holidays will be gradually extended also to collective farmers.

All-round measures to make working conditions healthier and lighter constitute an important task in improving the well-being of the people. Modern means of labor safety and hygiene designed to prevent occupational injuries and diseases will be introduced at all enterprises. Night shifts will be gradually abolished at enterprises, save those where round-the-clock operation is required by the production process or the need to service the population.

D. *Health services and measures for increased longevity.*

The socialist state is the only state which undertakes to protect and continuously improve the health of the whole population. This is provided for by a system of socio-economic and medical measures. There will be an extensive program designed to prevent and sharply reduce diseases, wipe out mass infectious diseases, and further increase longevity.

The needs of the urban and rural population in all forms of highly-qualified *medical services* will be met in full. This will call for the extensive building of medical institutions, including hospitals and sanatoria, the equipment of all medical institutions with modern appliances, and regular medical check-ups for the entire population. Special emphasis must be laid on extending in town and country the network of mother-and-child health institutions (maternity homes, medical consultation centers, children's health homes and hospitals, forest schools, etc.).

In addition to the existing free medical services, accommodation of sick persons at sanatoria and the dispensing of medicines will become gratuitous.

In order to afford the population an opportunity to rest in an out-of-town environment, holiday homes, boarding houses, country hotels, and tourist camps will be built, where working people will be acommodated at a reasonable charge or by way of a bonus, as well as at a discount or gratis.

The Party considers it a most important task to ensure the education from early childhood of a sound young generation, harmoniously developed physically and spiritually. This calls for utmost encouragement of all forms of mass sport and physical training, specifically at schools, and for drawing greater and greater sections of the population, particularly the youth, into sports.

E. *Improvement of family living conditions and of the position of women. Maintenance of children and incapacitated people at public expense.*

The remnants of the unequal position of women in domestic life must be totally eliminated. Social and living conditions must be provided to enable women to combine happy motherhood with increasingly active and creative participation in social labor and social activities, and in scientific and artistic pursuits. Women must be given relatively lighter and yet sufficiently well-paid jobs. Confinement leave will be extended.

It is essential to provide conditions to reduce and lighten the domestic work of women, and later to make possible the replacement of domestic work by public forms of satisfying the daily needs of the family. Up-to-date inexpensive domestic machinery, appliances, and electrical devices will be made extensively available for this purpose; the needs of the population in service establishments will be fully met in the next few years.

The extension of *public catering*, including canteens at enterprises, institutions, and in big dwelling houses, until it meets the demands of the population, calls for special attention. The service at catering establishments and the quality of catering must be radically improved, so that meals at public catering establishments should be tasty and nourishing and should cost the family less than meals cooked at home. Price reductions in public catering will keep ahead of price reductions for foodstuffs in the shops. By virtue of all this, public catering will be able to take precedence over home cooking within 10–15 years.

The transition to free public catering (midday meals) at enterprises and institutions, and for collective farmers at work, will begin in the second decade.

A happy childhood for every child is one of the most important and noble aspects of communist construction. The development of a ramified network of children's institutions will make it possible for more and more families, and in the second decade for every family, to keep children and adolescents free of charge at children's establishments if they so desire. The Party considers it essential that everything should be done to meet fully in the next few years the demand in children's pre-school institutions.

In town and country there will be: full and cost-free satisfaction of the population's need in nurseries, kindergartens, playgrounds, day-care schools and young pioneer camps; the mass provision of an extensive network of boarding schools with free maintenance of children; free hot meals at all schools, introduction of after-school hours with free dinners for school children, and free issue of uniforms and school supplies.

In keeping with the growth of the national income, the organs of state, the trade unions, and the kolkhozes in the course of the twenty years gradually will undertake maintenance of all citizens incapacitated through old age or some disability. Sickness and disability grants and old-age pensions will be extended to kolkhoz members; old-age and disability pensions will be raised steadily. The number of comfortable homes for old people and invalids providing free accommodation for all applicants will be greatly increased in town and country.

By fulfilling the tasks set by the Party for the improvement of the well-being of the people, the Soviet Union will make considerable headway towards the practical realization of the communsit principle of distribution according to need.

At the end of the twenty years public consumption funds will total about half of the aggregate real income of the population. This will make it possible to effect at public expense:

Free maintenance of children at children's institutions and boarding-schools (if parents wish).

Maintenance of disabled people.

Free education at all educational establishments.

Free medical services for all citizens, including the supply of medicines and the treatment of sick persons at sanatoria.

Rent-free housing and free communal services.

Free municipal transport facilities.

Free use of some types of public services.

Steady reduction of charges for, and, partially, free use of holiday homes, boarding-houses, tourist camps, and sports facilities.

Increasingly broad provision of the population with benefits, privileges, and scholarships (grants to unmarried mothers, mothers of many children, scholarships for students).

Gradual introduction of free public catering (midday meals) at enterprises and institutions, and for collective farmers at work.

The Soviet state will thus demonstrate to the world a truly full satisfaction of the growing material and cultural requirements of man. The living standard of Soviet people will improve all the faster, the faster the productive forces of the country develop and labor productivity grows, and the more broadly the creative energy of the Soviet people comes into play.

The set program can be fulfilled with success under conditions of peace. Complications in the international situation and the resultant necessity to increase defense expenditures may hold up the fulfilment of the plans for raising the living standard of the people. An enduring normalization of international relations, reduction of military expenditures and, in particular, the realization of general and complete disarmament under an appropriate agreement between countries, would make it possible greatly to surpass the plans for raising the people's living standard.

The fulfilment of the grand program of improving the living standard of the Soviet people will have a world-wide historic impact. The Party calls on the Soviet people to work perseveringly, with inspiration. Every one of the working people of the Soviet Union must do his duty in the building of a communist society and in the effort to fulfil the program for the improvement of the people's living standard.

III. The Tasks of the Party in the Spheres of State Development and the Further Promotion of Socialist Democracy

The dictatorship of the proletariat, born of the socialist revolution, played an epoch-making role by ensuring the victory of socialism in the USSR. In the course of socialist construction, however, it underwent changes. After the exploiting classes had been eliminated, the function of suppressing their resistance ceased to exist. The chief functions of the socialist state—organization of the economy, culture, and education—developed in full measure. The socialist state entered a new period of its development. The state began to grow over into a nation-wide organization of the working people of socialist society. Proletarian democracy was growing more and more into a socialist democracy of the people as a whole.

The working class is the only class in history that does not aim to perpetuate its power. Having brought about the complete and final victory of socialism—the first phase of communism—and the transition of society to the full-scale construction of communism, the dictatorship of the proletariat has fulfilled its historic mission and has ceased to be indispensable in the USSR from the point of view of the tasks of internal development. The state, which arose as a state of the dictatorship of the proletariat, has, in the new, contemporary stage, become a state of the entire people, an organ expressing the interests and will of the people as a whole. Since the working class is the foremost and best organized force of Soviet society, it plays a leading role also in the period of the full-scale construction of communism. The working class will have completed its role of leader of society after communism is built and classes disappear.

The party holds that the dictatorship of the working class will cease to be necessary before the state withers away. The state as an organization of the entire people will survive until the complete victory of communism. Expressing the will of the people, it must organize the building up of the material and technical basis of communism, and the transformation of socialist relations into communist relations, must exercise control over the measure of work and the measure of consumption, promote the people's welfare, protect the rights and freedoms of Soviet citizens, socialist law and order, and socialist property, instill in the people conscious discipline and a communist attitude to labor, guarantee the defense and security of the country, promote fraternal cooperation with the socialist countries, uphold world peace, and maintain normal relations with all countries.

All-round extension and perfection of socialist democracy, active participation of all citizens in the administration of the state, in the management of economic and cultural development, improvement of the government apparatus, and increased control over its activity by the people constitute the main direction in which socialist statehood develops in the period of the building of communism. As socialist democracy develops, the organs of state power will gradually be transformed into organs of public self-government. The Leninist principle of democratic centralism, which ensures the proper combination of centralized leadership with the maximum encouragement of local initiative, the extension of the rights of the Union republics and greater creative activity of the masses, will be promoted. It is essential to strengthen discipline, constantly control the activities of all the sections of the administrative apparatus, check the execution of the decisions and laws of the Soviet state and heighten the responsibility of every official for the strict and timely implementation of these laws.

1. THE SOVIETS AND DEVELOPMENT OF THE DEMOCRATIC PRINCIPLES OF GOVERNMENT

The role of the Soviets, which are an all-inclusive organization of the people embodying their unity, will grow as communist construction progresses. The Soviets, which combine the features of a government body and a mass organization of the people, operate more and more like social organizations, with the masses participating extensively and directly in their work.

The Party considers it essential to perfect the forms of popular representation and promote the democratic principles of the Soviet electoral system.

In nominating candidates for election to the Soviets, it is necessary to guarantee the widest and fullest discussion of the personal qualities and suitability of the candidates at meetings and in the press to ensure the election of the worthiest and most authoritative of them.

To improve the work of the Soviets and bring fresh forces into them, it is advisable that at least one-third of the total number of deputies to a Soviet should be elected anew each time so that *fresh millions of working people may learn to govern the state.*

The Party considers *systematic renewal of the leading bodies* necessary to bring a wider range of able persons into them and rule out abuses of authority by individual government officials. It is advisable to introduce the principle that the leading officials of the Union, republican, and local bodies should be elected to their offices, as a rule, for not more than three consecutive terms. In those cases when the personal qualifications of the official in question are generally believed to make his further activity within a leading body useful and necessary, his reelection may be allowed. His election shall be considered valid if not a simple majority, but not less than three-quarters of the votes are cast in his favor.

The Party regards the perfection of the principles of socialist democracy and their rigid observance as a most important task. It is necessary to ensure in full: regular accountability of Soviets and Deputies to their constituents and the right of the electorate to recall ahead of term Deputies who have not justified the confidence placed in them; publicity and the free and full discussion of all important questions of government and of economic and cultural development at the meetings of Soviets; regular accountability of executive government bodies to meetings of Soviets—from top to bottom; checking the work of these bodies and control over their activity; systematic discussion by the Soviets of questions raised by Deputies; criticism of shortcomings in the work of government, economic, and other organizations.

Every Deputy to a Soviet must take an active part in government affairs and carry on definite work. The role of the standing committees of the Soviets will become greater. The standing committees of the Supreme Soviets must systematically control the activities of ministries, departments, and economic councils; they must actively contribute to the implementation of the decisions adopted by the respective Supreme Soviets. To improve the work of the legislative bodies and increase control over the executive bodies, Deputies shall be periodically released from their regular employment for committee work.

An increasing number of questions which now come under the jurisdiction of the departments and sections of executive bodies must be gradually referred to the standing committees of the local Soviets for decision.

The rights of the local Soviets of Working People's Deputies (local self-government) will be extended. Local Soviets will make final decisions on all questions of local significance.

Special attention should be paid to the strengthening of government bodies at district level. As kolkhoz-cooperative and public property draw closer together, a single democratic body administering all enterprises, organizations and institutions at district level will gradually take shape.

The participation of social organizations and associations of the people in the legislative activity of the representative bodies of the Soviet state will be extended. The trade unions, the Young

Communist League and other mass organizations as represented by their all-Union and republican bodies must be given the right to take legislative initiative, that is, to propose draft laws.

Discussion by the people of draft laws and other decisions of both national and local significance must become the rule. The most important draft laws should be put to a nation-wide referendum.

The CPSU attaches great importance to improving the work of the government apparatus, which is largely responsible for the proper utilization of all the resources of the country and the timely settlement of all questions relating to the cultural and everyday needs of the people. The Soviet government apparatus must be simple, qualified, inexpensive, efficient and free of bureaucracy, formalism, and red tape.

Constant state and public control is an important means of accomplishing this task. In keeping with Lenin's directions, control bodies must function permanently to combine state control with public inspection at the center and in the localities. The Party regards inspection by people's control bodies as an effective means of drawing large sections of the people into the management of state affairs and control over the strict observance of legality, as a means of perfecting the government apparatus, eradicating bureaucracy, and promptly realizing proposals made by the people.

The government apparatus of the socialist state serves the people and is accountable to them. Negligence, abuse of power, and red tape by an official must be resolutely combated and the official concerned must be severely punished regardless of the position he holds. It is the duty of Soviet people to see to it that legality and law and order are rigidly enforced; they must not tolerate any abuses, and must combat them.

The Party holds that democratic principles in *administration* must be developed further. The principle of electivity and accountability to representative bodies and to the electorate will be gradually extended to all the leading officials of state bodies.

An effort should be made to ensure that the salaried government staffs are reduced, that ever larger sections of the people learn to take part in administration, and that work on government staffs eventually ceases to constitute a profession.

While every executive must be held strictly and personally responsible for the job entrusted to him, it is necessary consistently to exercise the principle of collective leadership at all levels of the government and economic apparatus.

The broadest democracy must go hand in hand with strict observance of comradely discipline by the working people, and should promote such discipline and control from above and from below. The important thing in the activity of all government bodies is organizational work among the masses, proper selection, testing, and appraisal of officials on the strength of their practical work, and control over the actual fulfilment of the assignments and decisions of the leading bodies.

The further *promotion of socialist law and order* and the improvement of legal rules governing economic organization, cultural, and educational work and contributing to the accomplishment of the tasks of communist construction and to the all-round development of the individual are very important.

The transition to communism means the fullest extension of personal freedom and the rights of Soviet citizens. Socialism has brought the working people the broadest guaranteed rights and freedoms. Communism will bring the working people further great rights and opportunities.

The Party's objective is to enforce strict observance of socialist legality, eradicate all violations of law and order, abolish crime, and remove all the causes of crime.

Justice in the USSR is exercised in full conformity with the law. It is based on truly democratic lines: election and accountability of the judges and people's assessors, the right to recall them before expiration of their term, the publicity of court proceedings, and the participation of prosecutors and advocates from the general public in the work of the courts, with the courts and investigating and prosecuting bodies strictly observing legality and all the norms of judicial procedure. The democratic foundation of justice will be developed and improved.

There should be no room for law-breakers and criminals in a society building communism. But as long as there are criminal offenses, it is necessary severely to punish those who commit crimes dangerous to society, violate the rules of the socialist community, and refuse to live by honest labor. Attention should be focussed mainly on crime prevention.

Higher standards of living and culture, and greater social consciousness of the people, pave the way to the abolition of crime and the ultimate replacement of judicial punishment by measures of public influence and education. Under socialism, anyone who has strayed from the path of the working man can return to useful activity.

The whole system of government and social organizations educates the people in a spirit of voluntary and conscientious fulfilment of their duties and leads to a natural fusion of rights and duties to form single standards of communist behavior.

2. THE FURTHER HEIGHTENING OF THE ROLE OF SOCIAL ORGANIZATIONS. THE STATE AND COMMUNISM

The role of social organizations increases in the period of the full-scale construction of communism. The *trade unions* acquire particular importance as schools of administration and economic management, as schools of communism. The Party will help the trade unions to take a growing share in economic management and to make the standing production conferences increasingly effective in improving the work of enterprises and exercising control over production. The trade unions shall:

Work constantly to increase the communist consciousness of the masses; organize an emulation movement for communist labor and help the working people in learning to manage state and social affairs; take an active part in controlling the measure of labor and the measure of consumption.

Encourage the activity of factory and office workers, enlisting their aid in the work for continuous technical progress, for higher productivity of labor, for the fulfilment and overfulfilment of state plans and assignments.

Work steadfastly for the improvement of the skill of factory and office workers and their working and living conditions; protect the material interests and rights of the working people.

Ensure that housing and cultural development plans are fulfilled and that public catering, trade, social insurance, and health resort services are improved.

Ensure control over the spending of public consumption funds and over the work of all enterprises and institutions serving the people.

Improve cultural services and recreation facilities for the working people; encourage physical training and sports.

The *Young Communist League*, an independently acting public organization of the youth which helps the Party to educate young people in a communist spirit, enlist them in the practical job of building the new society and train a generation of harmoniously developed people who will live, work and manage public affairs under communism, will play a greater role. The Party regards the youth as a great creative force in the Soviet people's struggle for communism.

The YCL must display still greater initiative in all spheres of life, must encourage the activity and labor heroism of the youth. YCL organizations must concentrate on educating the youth in a spirit of utmost devotion to their country, the people, the Communist Party and the communist cause, constant preparedness for labor for the good of society and for overcoming all difficulties and improving the general education and technical knowledge of all young men and women. It is the sacred duty of the YCL to prepare young people for the defense of their socialist country, to educate them as selfless patriots capable of firmly repelling any enemy. The YCL educates the youth in a spirit of strict adherence to communist moral principles and standards. Its activities in the schools and Young Pioneer organizations must contribute to the molding of a buoyant, industrious, and physically and morally sound generation.

A greater role will be played by *cooperatives*—kolkhozes, consumers', housing, and other cooperative organizations—as a form of drawing the masses into communist construction, as media of communist education and schools of public self-government.

Other social associations of the working people will likewise be developed—scientific, scientific-technical, and popular-science societies, rationalisers' and inventors' organizations, associations of writers, artists and journalists, cultural-education organizations, and sports societies.

The Party regards it as a major task of the social organizations to promote labor emulation in every possible way, and to encourage communist forms of labor, to stimulate the activity of working people in building a communist society, to work for the improvement of the living conditions of the people and the satisfaction of their growing spiritual requirements. Mass organizations should be given a greater part in managing cultural, health, and social insurance institutions; within the next few years they should be entrusted with the management of theaters and concert halls, clubs, libraries, and other state-controlled cultural-education establishments; they should be encouraged to play a greater part in promoting law and order, particularly through the people's volunteer squads and comradely courts.

To extend the independent activities of mass organizations, the Party considers it necessary further to reduce their salaried staffs from top to bottom, to renew each elective body by roughly as many as one-half of its membership at the regular election. It is advisable for the leading functionaries of social organizations not to be elected, as a general rule, for more than two consecutive terms.

As socialist statehood develops, it gradually will become *communist self-government* of the people which will embrace the Soviets, trade unions, cooperatives, and other mass organizations of the people. This process will represent a still greater development of democracy, ensuring the active participation of all members of society in the management of public affairs. Public functions similar to those performed by the state today in the sphere of economic and cultural management will be preserved under communism and will be modified and perfected as society develops. But the character of the functions and the ways in which they are carried out will be different from those under socialism. The bodies in charge of planning, accounting, economic management, and cultural advancement, now government bodies, will lose their political character and will become organs of public self-government. Communist society will be a highly-organized community of working men. Universally recognized rules of the communist way of life will be established whose observance will become an organic need and habit with everyone.

Historical development inevitably leads to the withering away of the state. To ensure that the state withers away completely, it is necessary to provide both internal conditions—the building of a developed communist society—and external conditions—the victory and consolidation of socialism in the world arena.

3. THE STRENGTHENING OF THE ARMED FORCES AND THE DEFENSE POTENTIAL OF THE SOVIET UNION

With the wholehearted support of the entire Soviet people, the Communist Party of the Soviet Union steadfastly upholds and defends the gains of socialism and the cause of world peace, and works tirelessly to deliver mankind for all time from wars of aggression. The Leninist principle of peaceful coexistence of states with different social systems always has been, and remains, the general principle of the foreign policy of the Soviet state.

The Soviet Union perseveringly seeks to bring about the realization of its proposals for general and complete disarmament under strict international control. But the imperialist countries stubbornly refuse to accept these proposals, and feverishly build up their armed forces. They refuse to reconcile themselves to the existence of the world socialist system, and openly proclaim their insane plans for the liquidation of the Soviet Union and the other socialist states through war. This obliges the Communist Party, the Armed Forces, the state security organs, and all the peoples of the USSR to be keenly vigilant with regard to the aggressive intrigues of the enemies of peace, always to protect peaceful labor, and constantly be prepared to take up arms in defense of their country.

The Party maintains that as long as imperialism exists the threat of aggressive wars will remain. The CPSU regards the defense of the socialist motherland, and the strengthening of the defense potential of the USSR, of the might of the Soviet Armed Forces, as a sacred duty of the Party and the Soviet people as a whole, as a most important function of the socialist state. The Soviet Union sees it as its internationalist duty to guarantee, together with the other socialist countries, the reliable defense and security of the entire socialist camp.

In terms of internal conditions, the Soviet Union needs no army. But since the danger of war coming from the imperialist camp persists, and since complete and general disarmament has not been achieved, the CPSU considers it necessary to maintain the defensive power of the Soviet state and the combat preparedness of its Armed Forces at a level ensuring the decisive and complete defeat of any enemy who dares to encroach upon the Soviet Union. The Soviet state will see to it that its Armed Forces are powerful, that they have the most up-to-date means of defending the country—atomic and thermonuclear weapons, rockets of every range—and that they keep all types of military equipment and all weapons up to standard.

The Party educates the Communists and all Soviet people in the spirit of constant prepardeness for the defense of their socialist country, of love of their armed forces. It will promote in every way the further development of voluntary mass defense organizations. Defense of the country, and service in the Soviet Armed Forces, is the lofty and honorable duty of Soviet citizens.

The CPSU is doing everything to ensure that the Soviet Armed Forces are a well-knit and smoothly operating organism, that they have a high standard of organization and discipline, carry out in exemplary fashion the tasks assigned them by the Party, the Government, the people, and are prepared at any moment to administer a crushing rebuff to imperialist aggressors. One-man leadership is a major principle of the organization of the Soviet Armed Forces.

The Party will work indefatigably to train Army and Navy officers and political and technical personnel fully devoted to the communist cause and recruited among the finest representatives of the Soviet people. It considers it necessary for the officer corps tirelessly to master Marxist-Leninist theory, to possess a high standard of military-technical training, meet all the requirements of modern military theory and practice, strengthen military discipline. All Soviet soldiers must be educated in the spirit of unqualified loyalty to the people, to the communist cause, of readiness to spare no effort and, if necessary, to give their lives in the defense of their socialist country.

Party leadership of the Armed Forces, and the increasing role and influence of the Party organizations in the Army and Navy are the bedrock of military development. The Party works unremittingly to increase its organizing and guiding influence on the entire life and activity of the Army, Air Force, and Navy, to rally the servicemen round the Communist Party and the Soviet Government, to strengthen the unity of the Armed Forces and the people, and to educate the soldiers in the spirit of courage, bravery, heroism, and comradeship with the armies of the socialist countries, of readiness at any moment to take up the defense of their Soviet country, which is building communism.

IV. The Tasks of the Party in the Field of National Relations

Under socialism the nations flourish and their sovereignty grows stronger. The development of nations does not proceed along lines of strengthening national strife, national narrow-mindedness and egoism, as it does under capitalism, but along lines of their association, fraternal mutual assistance, and friendship. The appearance of new industrial centers, the prospecting and development of mineral deposits, virgin land development, and the growth of all modes of transport increase the mobility of the population and promote greater intercourse between the peoples of the Soviet Union. People of many nationalities live together and work in harmony in the Soviet republics. The boundaries between the Union republics of the USSR increasingly are losing their former significance, since all the nations are equal, their life is based on a common socialist foundation, the material and spiritual needs of every people are satisfied to the same extent, and they are all united in a single family by common vital interests and are advancing together to the common goal, communism. Spiritual features deriving from the new type of social relations and embodying the finest traditions of the peoples of the

USSR have taken shape and are common to Soviet men and women of different nationalities.

Full-scale communist construction constitutes a new stage in the development of national relations in the USSR in which the nations will draw still closer together until complete unity is achieved. The building of the material and technical basis of communism leads to still greater unity of the Soviet peoples. The exchange of material and spiritual values between nations becomes more and more intensive, and the contribution of each republic to the common cause of communist construction increases. Obliteration of distinctions between classes and the development of communist social relations make for a greater social homogeneity of nations and contribute to the development of common communist traits in their culture, morals and way of living, to a further strengthening of their mutual trust and friendship.

With the victory of communism in the USSR, the nations will draw still closer together, their economic and ideological unity will increase, and the communist traits common to their spiritual make-up will develop. However, the obliteration of national distinctions, and especially of language distinctions, is a considerably longer process than the obliteration of class distinctions.

The Party approaches all questions of national relationships arising in the course of communist construction from the standpoint of proletarian internationalism and firm pursuance of the Leninist nationalities policy. The Party neither ignores nor over-accentuates national characteristics.

The Party sets the following tasks in the sphere of national relations:

(a) To continue the all-round economic and cultural development of all the Soviet nations and nationalities, ensuring their increasingly close fraternal cooperation, mutual aid, unity and affinity in all spheres of life, thus achieving the utmost strengthening of the Union of Soviet Socialist Republics; to make full use of, and advance the forms of, national statehood of the peoples of the USSR.

(b) In the economic sphere, it is necessary to continue the line of comprehensive development of the economies of the Soviet republics, effect a rational geographic location of production and a planned working of natural wealth, and promote socialist division of labor among the republics, unifying and combining their economic efforts, and properly balancing the interests of the state as a whole and those of each Soviet republic. The extension of the rights of the Union republics in economic management having produced substantial positive results, such measures may also be carried out in the future with due regard to the fact that the creation of the material and technical basis of communism will call for still greater interconnection and mutual assistance between the Soviet republics. The closer the intercourse between the nations and the greater the awareness of the country-wide tasks, the more successfully can manifestations of parochialism and national egoism be overcome.

In order to ensure the successful accomplishment of the tasks of communist construction and the coordination of economic activities, inter-republican economic organs may be set up in some zones (notably for such matters as irrigation, power grids, transport, etc.).

The Party will continue its policy ensuring the actual equality of all nations and nationalities with full consideration for their interests and devoting special attention to those areas of the country which are in need of more rapid development. Benefits accumulating in the course of communist construction must be fairly distributed among all nations and nationalities.

(c) To work for the further all-round development of the socialist cultures of the peoples of the USSR. The big scale of communist construction and the new victories of communist ideology are enriching the cultures of the peoples of the USSR, which are socialist in content and national in form. There is a growing ideological unity among the nations and nationalities and a greater *rapprochement* of their cultures. The historical experience of socialist nations shows that national forms do not ossify; they change, advance, and draw closer together, shedding all outdated traits that contradict the new conditions of life. An international culture common to all the Soviet nations is developing. The cultural treasures of each nation are increasingly augmented by works acquiring an international character.

Attaching decisive importance to the development of the socialist content of the cultures of the peoples of the USSR, the Party will promote their further mutual enrichment and rapprochement, the consolidation of their international basis, and thereby the formation of the future single world-wide culture of communist society. While supporting the progressive traditions of each people, and making them the property of all Soviet people, the Party will in all ways further new revolutionary traditions of the builders of communism common to all nations.

(d) To continue promoting the free development of the languages of the peoples of the USSR and the complete freedom for every citizen of the USSR to speak, and to bring up and educate his children, in any language, ruling out all privileges, restrictions or compulsions in the use of this or that language. By virtue of the fraternal friendship and mutual trust of peoples, national languages are developing on a basis of equality and mutual enrichment.

The voluntary study of Russian in addition to the native language is of positive significance, since it facilitates reciprocal exchanges of experience and access of every nation and nationality to the cultural gains of all the other peoples of the USSR and to world culture. The Russian language has, in effect, become the common medium of intercourse and cooperation between all the peoples of the USSR.

(e) To pursue consistently as heretofore the principles of internationalism in the field of national relations; to strengthen the friendship of peoples as one of the most important gains of socialism; to conduct a relentless struggle against manifestations and survivals of nationalism and chauvinism of all types, against trends of national narrow-mindedness and exclusiveness, idealization of the past and the veiling of social contradictions in the history of peoples, and against customs and habits hampering communist construction. The growing scale of communist construction calls for the continuous exchange of trained personnel among nations. Manifestations of national aloofness in the education and employment of workers of different nationalities in the Soviet republics are impermissible. The elimination of manifestations of nationalism is in the interests of all nations and nationalities of the USSR. Every Soviet republic can continue to flourish and strengthen only in the great family of fraternal socialist nations of the USSR.

V. The Tasks of the Party in the Spheres of Ideology, Education, Instruction, Science, and Culture

Soviet society has made great progress in the socialist education of the masses, in the molding of active builders of socialism. But even after the socialist system has triumphed there persist in the minds and behavior of people survivals of capitalism, which hamper the progress of society.

In the struggle for the victory of communism, ideological work becomes an increasingly powerful factor. The higher the social consciousness of the members of society, the more fully and broadly their creative activities come into play in the building of the material and technical basis of communism, in the development of communist forms of labor and new relations between people, and, consequently, the more rapidly and successfully the building of communism proceeds.

The Party considers that the paramount task in the ideological field in the present period is to educate all working people in a spirit of ideological integrity and devotion to communism, and cultivate in them a communist attitude to labor and the social economy; to eliminate completely the survivals of bourgeois views and morals; to ensure the all-round, harmonious development of the individual; to create a truly rich spiritual culture. Special importance is attached by the Party to the molding of the rising generation.

The molding of the new man is effected through his own active participation in communist construction and the development of communist principles in the economic and social spheres, under the influence of the educational work carried out by the Party, the state, and various social organizations, work in which the press, radio, cinema, and television play an important part. As communist forms of social organization are created, communist ideas will become more firmly rooted in life and work and in human relations, and people will develop the ability to enjoy the benefits of communism in a rational way. Joint planned labor by the members of society, their daily participation in the management of state and public affairs, and the development of communist relations of comradely cooperation and mutual support, recast the minds of people in a spirit of collectivism, industry, and humanism.

Increased communist consciousness of the people furthers the ideological and political unity of the workers, collective farmers, and intellectuals and promotes their gradual fusion in the single collective of the working people of communist society.

The Party sets the following tasks:

1. IN THE FIELD OF DEVELOPMENT OF COMMUNIST CONSCIOUSNESS

A. *The shaping of a scientific world outlook.*

Under socialism and at a time when a communist society is being built, when spontaneous economic development has given way to the conscious organization of production and social life as a whole, and when theory is daily translated into practice, it is of prime importance that a scientific world outlook be shaped in all working people of Soviet society on the basis of Marxism-Leninism, an integral and harmonious system of philosophical, economic, and socio-political views. The Party calls for the education of the population as a whole in the spirit of scientific communism and strives to ensure that all working people fully understand the course and perspective of world development, that they take a correct view of international and domestic events, and consciously build their life on communist lines. Communist ideas and communist deeds should blend organically in the behavior of every person and in the activities of all collectives and organizations.

The theoretical elaboration and timely practical solution of new problems raised by life are essential to the successful advance of society to communism. Theory must continue to illumine the road of practice, and help detect and eliminate obstacles and difficulties hindering successful communist construction. The Party regards it as one of its most important duties further to elaborate Marxist-Leninist theory by studying and generalizing new phenomena in the life of Soviet society and in the experience of the world revolutionary working-class and liberation movements, and creatively to combine the theory and the practice of communist construction.

B. *Labor education.*

The Party sees the development of a communst attitude to labor in all members of society as its chief educational task. Labor for the benefit of society is the sacred duty of all. Any labor for society, whether physical or mental, is honorable and commands respect. Exemplary labor and management in the social economy should serve to educate all working people.

Everything required for life and human progress is created by labor. Hence every able-bodied man must take part in creating the means which are indispensable for his life and work and for the welfare of society. Anyone who received any benefits from society without doing his share of work, would be a parasite living at the expense of others.

It is impossible for a man in communist society not to work, for neither his social consciousness nor public opinion would permit it. Work according to one's ability will become a habit, a prime necessity of life, for every member of society.

C. *The affirmation of communist morality.*

In the course of transition to communism, the moral principles of society become increasingly important; the sphere of action of the moral factor expands and the importance of the administrative control of human relations diminishes accordingly. The Party will encourage all forms of conscious civic self-discipline leading to the assertion and promotion of the basic rules of the communist way of life.

The Communists reject the class morality of the exploiters; in contrast to the perverse, selfish views and morals of the old world, they promote communist morality, which is the noblest and most just morality, for it expresses the interests and ideals of the whole of working mankind. Communism makes the elementary standards of morality and justice, which were distorted or shamelessly flouted under the rule of the exploiters, inviolable rules for relations both between individuals and between peoples. Communist morality encompasses the fundamental norms of human morality which the masses of the people evolved in the course of millenniums as they fought against vice and social oppression. The revolutionary morality of the working class is of particular importance to the moral advancement of society. As socialist and communist construction progresses, communist morality is enriched with new principles, a new content.

The Party holds that *the moral code of the builder of communism* should comprise the following principles:

Devotion to the communist cause; love of the socialist motherland and of the other socialist countries.

Conscientious labor for the good of society—he who does not work, neither shall he eat.

Concern on the part of everyone for the preservation and growth of public wealth.

A high sense of public duty; intolerance of actions harmful to the public interest.

Collectivism and comradely mutual assistance: one for all and all for one.

Humane relations and mutual respect between individuals—man is to man a friend, comrade and brother.

Honesty and truthfulness, moral purity, modesty, and unpretentiousness in social and private life.

Mutual respect in the family, and concern for the upbringing of children.

An uncompromising attitude to injustice, parasitism, dishonesty, careerism, and money-grubbing.

Friendship and brotherhood among all peoples of the USSR; intolerance of national and racial hatred.

An uncompromising attitude to the enemies of communism, peace, and the freedom of nations.

Fraternal solidarity with the working people of all countries, and with all peoples.

D. *The promotion of proletarian internationalism and socialist patriotism.*

The Party untiringly will educate Soviet people in the spirit of proletarian internationalism and will promote vigorously the international solidarity of the working people. In fostering the Soviet people's love of their country, the Party maintains that with the emergence of the world socialist system the patriotism of the members of socialist society is expressed in devotion and loyalty to their own country and to the entire community of socialist countries. Socialist patriotism and socialist internationalism necessarily imply proletarian solidarity with the working class and all working people of all countries. The Party will continue perseveringly to combat the reactionary ideology of bourgeois nationalism, racism, and cosmopolitanism.

E. *All-round and harmonious development of the individual.*

In the period of transition to communism, there are greater opportunities of *educating a new man, who will combine harmoniously spiritual wealth, moral purity, and a perfect physique.*

All-round development of the individual has been made possible by historic social gains—freedom from exploitation, unemployment and poverty, from discrimination on account of sex, origin, nationality or race. Every member of society is provided with equal opportunities for education and creative labor. Relations of dependence and inequality between people in public affairs and in family life disappear. The personal dignity of each citizen is protected by society. Each is guaranteed an equal and free choice of occupation and profession with due regard to the interests of society. As less and less time is spent on material production, the individual is afforded ever greater opportunities to develop his abilities, gifts, and talents in the fields of production, science, engineering, literature, and the arts. People increasingly will devote their leisure to public pursuits, cultural intercourse, intellectual and physical development, scientific, technical and artistic endeavor. Physical training and sports will become part and parcel of the everyday life of people.

F. *Elimination of the survivals of capitalism in the minds and behavior of people.*

The Party considers it an integral part of its communist education work to combat manifestations of bourgeois ideology and morality, and the remnants of private-owner psychology, superstitions, and prejudices.

The general public, public opinion, and extensive criticism and self-criticism must play a big role in combating survivals of the past and manifestations of individualism and selfishness. Comradely censure of anti-social behavior gradually will become the principal means of doing away with manifestations of bourgeois views, customs, and habits. The power of example in public affairs and in private life, in the performance of one's public duty, acquires tremendous educational significance.

The Party uses ideological media to educate people in the spirit of a scientific materialist world conception, to overcome religious prejudices without insulting the sentiments of believers. It is necessary to conduct regularly broad atheistic propaganda on a scientific basis, to explain patiently the untenability of religious beliefs, which were engendered in the past when people were overawed by the elemental forces and social oppression, and did not know the real causes of natural and social phenomena. This can be done by making use of the achievements of modern science, which is solving steadily the mysteries of the universe and extending man's power over nature, leaving no room for religious inventions about supernatural forces.

G. *The exposure of bourgeois ideology.*

The peaceful coexistence of states with different social systems does not imply any easing of the ideological struggle. The Communist Party will go on *exposing the anti-popular, reactionary nature of capitalism* and all attempts to paint bright pictures of the capitalist system.

The Party will *steadfastly propagate the great advantages of socialism and communism over the declining capitalist system.*

The Party advances the scientific ideology of communism in contrast to reactionary bourgeois ideology. Communist ideology, which expresses the fundamental interests of the working class and all working people, teaches them to struggle, to live and work, for the happiness of all. It is the most humane ideology. Its ideals are to establish truly human relations between individuals and peoples, to deliver mankind from the threat of wars of extermination, and bring about universal peace and a free, happy life for all men on earth.

2. IN THE FIELD OF PUBLIC EDUCATION

The transition to communism implies training that will make people communist-minded and highly cultured, people fitted for both physical and mental labor, for active work in various social, governmental, scientific, and cultural spheres.

The system of public education is so organized as to ensure that the instruction and education of the rising generation are closely bound up with life and productive labor, and that the adult population can combine work in the sphere of production with further training and education in keeping with their vocations and the requirements of society. Public education along these lines will make for the molding of harmoniously developed members of communist society and for the solution of a cardinal social problem, namely, the elimination of substantial distinctions between mental and physical labor.

The main tasks in the field of instruction and education are:

A. *Introduction of universal compulsory secondary education.*

In the next decade compulsory secondary general and polytechnical eleven-year education is to be introduced for all children of school age, and eight-year education for young people engaged in the national economy who have not had the appropriate schooling; in the subsequent decade every one will have the opportunity to receive a complete secondary education. Universal secondary education is guaranteed by the development of general and polytechnical education, professional training combined with socially useful labor of school children to the extent of their physical capacity, and a considerable expansion of the network of all types of general schools, including evening schools, which provide a secondary education in off-work hours.

Secondary education must furnish a solid knowledge of the fundamentals of the basic sciences, an understanding of the principles of the communist world outlook, and a labor and polytechnical training in accordance with the rising level of science and engineering, with due regard to the needs of society and to the abilities and inclinations of the students, as well as the moral, esthetic, and physical education of a healthy rising generation.

In view of the rapid progress of science and engineering, the system of industrial, professional, and vocational training should be improved continuously, so that the skills of those engaged in production may develop together with their better general education in the social and natural sciences and with the acquisition of specialized knowledge in engineering, agronomy, medicine, and other fields.

B. *The public upbringing of children of pre-school and school age.*

The communist system of public education is based on the public upbringing of children. The educational influence which the family exerts on children must be brought into ever greater harmony with their public upbringing.

The growing number of pre-school institutions and boarding-schools of different types will fully meet the requirements of all working people who wish to give their children of pre-school and school age a public upbringing. The importance of the school, which is to cultivate love of labor and knowledge in children and to raise the younger generation in the spirit of communist consciousness and morality, will increase. An honorable and responsible role in this respect falls to teachers, and to the Komsomol and Young Pioneer organizations.

C. *Creation of conditions for high-standard instruction and education of the rising generation.*

The Party plans to carry out an extensive program for the construction of schools and cultural-education establishments to meet fully the needs of education and instruction. All schools will be housed in good buildings and will go over to a one-shift time-table. They will all have study workshops and chemical, physical, and other laboratories; rural schools will also have their own farming plots; large factories will have production training shops for school children. Modern facilities—cinema, radio, and television—will be used widely in schools.

For physical training and esthetic education, all schools and extra-scholastic establishments will have gymnasiums, sports grounds, and facilities for the creative endeavor of children in music, painting, sculpture, etc. The network of sports schools, sports grounds, tourist camps, skiing centers, aquatic stations, swimming pools, and other sports facilities will be expanded in town and countryside.

D. *Higher and secondary special education.*

In step with scientific and technical progress, higher and secondary special education, which must train highly-skilled specialists with a broad theoretical and political background, will be expanded.

Shorter working hours and a considerable improvement in the standard of living of the entire population will provide everyone with an opportunity to receive a higher or secondary special education if he so desires. The number of higher and secondary specialized schools, evening and correspondence schools in particular, as well as higher schools at factories, agricultural institutes (on large state farms), studios, conservatories, etc., must be increased in all areas of the country with the support of factories and trade unions and other social organizations. The plan is to increase considerably every year the number of students at higher and secondary specialized schools; special education will be afforded to tens of millions of people.

3. IN THE FIELD OF SCIENCE

Under the socialist system of economy, scientific and technical progress enables man to employ the riches and forces of nature most effectively in the interests of the people, to discover new forms of energy and to create new materials, to develop means of weather control, and to master outer space. Application of science in production becomes a decisive factor of rapid growth of the productive forces of society. Scientific progress and the introduction of scientific achievements into the economy will remain an object of special concern to the Party.

Most important are the following tasks:

A. *Development of theoretical investigations.*

The further perspectives of scientific and technical progress depend in the present period primarily on the achievements of *the key branches of natural science.* A high level of development in *mathematics, physics, chemistry, and biology* is a necessary condition for the advancement and the effectiveness of the technical, medical, agricultural, and other sciences.

Theoretical research will be promoted to the utmost, primarily in such decisive fields of technical progress as electrification of the whole country, comprehensive mechanization and automation of production, transport and communications, the application of chemistry to the leading branches of the national economy, industrial uses of atomic energy. This applies to:

Studying the power and fuel balance of the country, finding the best ways and means of utilizing the natural sources of power, working out the scientific fundamentals of a single power grid, discovering new power sources and developing methods of direct conversion of thermal, nuclear, solar, and chemical energy into electric power, and solving problems related to control of thermonuclear reactions.

Working out the theory and principles of designing new machines, automatic and telemechanical systems, intensively developing radioelectronics, elaborating the theoretical foundations of computing, control and information machines, and technically improving them.

Investigating chemical processes, working out new, more efficient technologies and creating inexpensive high-quality artificial and synthetic materials for all branches of the national economy: mechanical engineering, building, and the manufacture of household goods and mineral fertilizers, and creating new preparations for use in medicine and agriculture.

Improving existing methods and devising new, more effective

methods of prospecting minerals and making comprehensive use of natural wealth.

Big advances are to be made in the development of all the biological sciences in order successfully to solve medical problems and achieve further progress in agriculture. The main tasks to be solved by these sciences in the interests of mankind are: ascertainment of the essence of the phenomena of life, the biological laws governing the development of the organic world, study of the physics and chemistry of living matter, elaboration of various methods of controlling vital processes, in particular, metabolism, heredity and directed changes in organisms. It is essential to develop more broadly and deeply the Michurin line in biology, which is based on the proposition that conditions of life are primary in the development of the organic world. Medicine must concentrate on discovering means of preventing and conquering cancer, virulent, cardio-vascular, and other dangerous diseases. It is important to study and extensively use microorganisms in the economy and the health services, among other things for the production of foods and feedstuffs, vitamins, antibiotics and enzymes, and for the development of new agricultural techniques.

Artificial earth satellites and spaceships, by enabling man to penetrate into outer space, have provided great opportunities for discovering new natural phenomena and laws and for investigating the planets and the sun.

In the age of rapid scientific progress, the elaboration of the philosophical problems of modern natural science on the basis of dialectical materialism, the only scientific method of cognition, becomes still more urgent.

There must be intensive development of research work in the *social sciences,* which constitute the scientific basis for the guidance of the development of society. Most important in this field is the study and theoretical generalization of the experience gained in communist construction; investigation of the key objective laws governing the economic, political, and cultural progress of socialism and its development into communism, and elaboration of the problems of communist education.

The task of economic science is to generalize new phenomena in the economic life of society, and to work out the national economic problems whose solution promotes successful communist construction. Economists must concentrate on finding the most effective ways of utilizing material and labor resources in the economy, the best methods of planning and organizing industrial and agricultural production, and elaborating the principles of a rational distribution of the productive forces and of the technical and economic problems of communist construction.

The investigation of the problems of world history and contemporary world development must disclose the law-governed process and mankind's advance towards communism, the change in the balance of forces in favor of socialism, the aggravation of the general crisis of capitalism, the breakup of the colonial system of imperialism and its consequences, and the upsurge of the national liberation movement of peoples.

It is important to study the historical experience of the Communist Party and the Soviet people, tried and proved successful in practice, the objective laws of development of the world socialist system and the world Communist and working-class movement.

It is essential, in the future as well, firmly to defend and develop dialectical and historical materialism as the science of the most general laws of development of nature, society, and human thinking.

The social sciences must continue to struggle with determination against bourgeois ideology, against Right-Socialist theory and practice, and against revisionism and dogmatism; they must uphold the purity of the principles of Marxism-Leninism.

B. *Ties between science and production.*

Close ties with the creative labor of the people and practical communist construction are an earnest of a fruitful development of science.

In conformity with the requirements of economic and cultural development, it is essential to extend and improve the network of research institutions, including those attached to the central bodies directing economic development and those attached to the economic councils, and the network of research laboratories and institutes at the major industrial plants and in farming areas; to develop research at higher educational establishments; to improve the geographical distribution of research institutions and higher educational establishments, and to ensure the further development of science in all the Union republics and major economic areas.

The research institutions must plan and coordinate their work in the most important fields of research in accordance with the plans of economic and cultural development. The role of the collective opinion of scientists in directing scientific work will increase. Free comradely discussions promoting the creative solution of pressing problems are an essential condition for scientific development.

The Party will adopt measures to extend and improve the material facilities of science and to enlist the most capable creative forces in scientific pursuits.

It is a point of honor for Soviet scientists to consolidate the advanced positions which Soviet science has won in major branches of knowledge and to take *a leading place in world science* in all the key fields.

4. IN THE FIELD OF CULTURAL DEVELOPMENT, LITERATURE AND ART

Cultural development during the full-scale construction of communist society will constitute the closing stage of a great cultural revolution. At this stage all the necessary ideological and cultural conditions will be created for the victory of communism.

The growth of the productive forces, progress in engineering and in the organization of production, increased social activity of the working people, development of the democratic principles of self-government, and a communist reorganization of everyday life depend in very large measure on the cultural advancement of the population.

Absorbing and developing all the best that has been created by world culture, communist culture will be a new, higher stage in the cultural progress of mankind. It will embody the versatility and richness of the spiritual life of society, and the lofty ideals and humanism of the new world. It will be the culture of a classless society, a culture of the entire people, of all mankind.

A. *All-round advancement of the cultural life of society.*

In the period of transition to communism, creative effort in all fields of culture becomes particularly fruitful and accessible to all members of society. Soviet literature, music, painting, cinema and theater, television and all the other arts, will attain higher standards in their ideological make-up and artistry. People's theaters, mass amateur art, technical invention, and other forms of creative endeavor by the people will become widespread. The advancement of artistic and creative activities among the masses will ensure the appearance of new gifted writers, artists, musicians, and actors. The development and enrichment of the arts are based on a combination of mass amateur endeavor and professional art.

The Party will work unremittingly to ensure that literature, art, and culture flourish, that every individual is given full scope to apply his abilities, that the people are educated esthetically and develop a fine artistic taste and cultural habits. The artistic element will ennoble labor still more, make living conditions more attractive, and lift man up spiritually.

To provide the material basis for cultural development on a grand scale:

Book publishing and the press will be vigorously developed, and the printing and paper industries will be expanded accordingly.

There will be more libraries, lecture halls and reading-rooms, theaters, houses of culture, clubs, and cinemas.

The country-wide radio diffusion network will be completed; television stations covering all industrial and agricultural areas will be built.

People's unversities, people's theatrical companies, and other amateur cultural organizations will be developed widely.

A large network of scientific and technical laboratories and of art and cinema studios will be provided for the use of all who have the inclination and ability.

The Party considers it necessary to distribute cultural institutions evenly throughout the country in order gradually to bring the cultural standard of the countryside level with that of the town and achieve rapid cultural progress in all the newly-developed areas.

B. *Enhancement of the educational role of literature and art.*

Soviet literature and art, imbued with optimism and dynamic communist ideas, are great factors in ideological education and cultivate in Soviet people the qualities of builders of a new world. They must be a source of joy and inspiration to millions of people, express their will, their sentiments and ideas, enrich them ideologically and educate them morally.

The highroad of literature and art lies through the strengthening of their bond with the life of the people, through faithful and highly artistic depiction of the richness and versatility of socialist reality, inspired and vivid portrayal of all that is new and genuinely communist, and exposure of all that hinders the progress of society.

In the art of socialist realism, which is based on the principles of partisanship and kinship with the people, bold pioneering in the artistic depiction of life goes hand in hand with the cultivation and development of the progressive traditions of world culture. Writers, artists, musicians, theatrical workers, and film makers have every opportunity of displaying creative initiative and skill, using manifold forms, styles, and genres.

The Communist Party shows solicitude for the proper development of literature and art and their ideological and artistic standards, helps social organizations and literary and art associations in their activities.

C. *The expansion of international cultural relations.*

The Party considers it necessary to expand the Soviet Union's cultural relations with the countries of the socialist system and with all other countries for the purpose of pooling scientific and cultural achievements and of bringing about mutual understanding and friendship among the peoples.

VI. Communist Construction in the USSR and Cooperation of the Socialist Countries

The CPSU regards communist construction in the Soviet Union as a component of the building of communist society by the peoples of the entire world socialist system.

The fact that socialist revolutions took place at different times and that the economic and cultural levels of the countries concerned are dissimilar, predetermines the non-simultaneous completion of socialist construction in those countries and their non-simultaneous entry into the period of the full-scale construction of communism. Nevertheless, the fact that the socialist countries are developing as members of a single world socialist system and utilizing the objective laws and advantages of this system *enables them to reduce the time necessary for the construction of socialism and offers them the prospect of effecting the transition to communism more or less simultaneously, within one and the same historical epoch.*

The first country to advance to communism facilitates and accelerates the advance of the entire world socialist system to communism. In building communism, the peoples of the Soviet Union are breaking new roads for mankind, testing their correctness by their own experience, bringing out difficulties, finding ways and means of overcoming them, and selecting the best forms and methods of communist construction.

Since the social forces—the working class, the cooperative peasantry, and the people's intelligentsia—and the social forms of economy (enterprises based on the two forms of socialist property) in the Soviet Union and in the other socialist countries are of one type, there will be common basic objective laws for communist construction in the USSR and in those countries, with due allowance made for the historical and national peculiarities of each country.

The construction of communism in the USSR promotes the interests of every country of the socialist community, for it increases the economic might and defense potential of the world socialist camp and provides progressively favorable opportunities for the USSR to expand its economic and cultural cooperation with the other socialist countries and increase the assistance and support it renders them.

The CPSU maintains that the existing forms of economic relations between the socialist countries—foreign trade, coordination of economic plans, and specialization and combination of production—will be developed and perfected more and more.

The socialist system makes possible the abolition of the disparities in the economic and cultural development of countries inherited from capitalism, the more rapid development of the countries whose economy lagged behind under capitalism, the steady promotion of their economies and cultures with the purpose of evening up the general level of development of the countries of the socialist community. This is ensured by the advantages of the socialist economic system and by equality in economic relations; by mutual assistance and the sharing of experience, specifically, by reciprocal exchanges of scientific and technological achievements and by coordinated research; by the joint construction of industrial projects and by cooperation in the development of natural resources. All-round fraternal cooperation benefits every socialist country and the world socialist system as a whole.

It is in the best interest of socialist and communist construction that each socialist country combines the effort to strengthen and develop its national economy with the effort to expand economic cooperation of the socialist community as a whole. The development and leveling of the economy of the socialist countries must be achieved primarily by every country using its internal resources to the full, by improving the forms and methods of economic leadership, steadily applying the Leninist principles and methods of socialist economic management, and making effective use of the advantages of the world socialist system.

Material prerequisites for the construction of communism are created by the labor of the people of the country concerned and by its steadily growing contribution to the common cause—the consolidation of the socialist system. This purpose is served by the application in socialist construction of the law of planned, proportionate development; encouragement of the creative initiative and labor activity of the masses; continuous perfection of the system of the international division of labor through the coordination of national economic plans, specialization and combination of production within the world socialist system on the basis of voluntary participation, mutual benefit and an overall improvement of the level of science and engineering; the study of collective experience; the promotion of cooperation and fraternal mutual assistance; strict adherence to the principles of material incentive and the all-round promotion of moral stimuli to work for the good of society; control over the measure of labor and rate of consumption.

Socialism brings peoples and countries together. In the course of extensive cooperation in all economic, socio-political and cultural fields, the common economic basis of world socialism will be consolidated.

The objective laws of the world socialist system, the growth of the productive forces of socialist society, and the vital interests of the peoples of the socialist countries predetermine an increasing affinity of the various national economies. As Lenin foresaw, tendencies develop toward the future creation of a world communist economy regulated by the victorious working people according to one single plan.

The CPSU, in community with the Communist parties of the other socialist countries, regards the following as its tasks:

In the *political* field, the utmost strengthening of the world socialist system; promotion of fraternal relations with all the socialist countries on lines of complete equality and voluntary cooperation; political consolidation of the countries of the socialist community for joint struggle against imperialist aggressors, for universal peace and for the complete triumph of communism.

In the *economic* field, expansion of trade between the socialist countries; development of the international socialist division of labor; increasing coordination of long-range economic plans of the socialist countries to ensure a maximum saving of social labor and an accelerated development of the world socialist economy; the promotion of scientific and technical cooperation.

In the *cultural* field, steady development of all forms of cultural cooperation and intercourse between the peoples of the socialist countries; exchanges of cultural achievements; encouragement of joint creative effort by scientists, writers, and artists; extensive measures to ensure the mutual enrichment of national cultures and bring the mode of life and the spiritual cast of the socialist nations closer together.

The CPSU and the Soviet people will do evertyhing in their power to support all the peoples of the socialist community in the construction of socialism and communism.

VII. The Party in the Period of Full-Scale Communist Construction

As a result of the victory of socialism in the USSR and the consolidation of the unity of Soviet society, the Communist Party of the working class has become the vanguard of the Soviet people, a Party of the entire people, and extended its guiding influence to all spheres of social life. The Party is the brain, the honor and the conscience of our epoch, of the Soviet people, the people effecting great revolutionary transformations. It looks keenly into the future and shows the people scientifically-motivated roads along which to advance, arouses titanic energy in the masses, and leads them to the accomplishment of great tasks.

The period of full-scale communist construction is characterized by a further *enhancement of the role and importance of the Communist Party* as the leading and guiding force of Soviet society.

Unlike all the preceding socio-economic formations, communist society does not develop spontaneously, but as a result of the conscious and purposeful efforts of the masses led by the Marxist-Leninist Party. The Communist Party, which unites the foremost representatives of the working class, of all working people, and is closely connected with the masses, which enjoys unbounded prestige among the people and understands the laws of social development, provides proper leadership in communist construction as a whole, giving it an organized, planned and scientifically based character.

The enhancement of the role of the Party in the life of Soviet society in the new stage of its development derives from:

The growing scope and complexity of the tasks of communist construction, which call for a higher level of political and organizational leadership.

The growth of the creative activity of the masses and the participation of fresh millions of working people in the administration of state affairs and of production.

The further development of socialist democracy, the enhancement of the role of social organizations, the extension of the rights of the Union republics and local organizations.

The growing importance of the theory of scientific communism, of its creative development and propaganda, the necessity for improving the communist education of the working people and struggling to overcome the survivals of the past in the minds of people.

There must be a new, higher stage in the development of the Party itself and of its political, ideological, and organizational work that is in conformity with the full-scale building of communism. The Party will improve continuously the forms and methods of its work, so that its leadership of the masses, of the building of the material and technical basis of communism, of the development of society's spiritual life will keep pace with the growing requirements of the epoch of communist construction.

Being the vanguard of the people building a communist society, the Party must also be in the van in the organization of internal Party life and serve as an example and model in developing the most advanced forms of public communist self-government.

Undeviating observance of the Leninist standards of Party life and the principle of collective leadership, enhancement of the responsibility of Party organs and their personnel to the Party rank and file, promotion of the activity and initiative of all Communists and of their participation in elaborating and realizing the policy of the Party, and the development of criticism and self-criticism, are a law of Party life. This is an imperative condition of the ideological and organizational strength of the Party itself, of the unity and solidarity of Party ranks, of an all-round development of inner-Party democracy and an activization on this basis of all Party forces, and of the strengthening of ties with the masses.

The cult of the individual, and the violations of collectivism in leadership, of inner-Party democracy and socialist legality arising out of it, are incompatible with the Leninist principles of Party life. The cult of the individual belittles the role of the Party and the masses and hampers the development of the ideological life of the Party and the creative activity of the working people.

In order to effect the Leninist principle of collective leadership consistently, to ensure a greater influx of fresh Party forces into the leading Party organs, to combine properly old and young cadres, and to rule out the possibility of an excessive concentration of power in the hands of individual officials and prevent cases of their getting beyond the control of the collective, the Party considers it necessary to carry out the following measures:

(a) To introduce in practice a regular renewal, in certain proportions, of the members of all elected Party bodies—from primary organizations to the Central Committee, at the same time preserving continuity of leadership.

At all regular elections, not less than one-quarter of the members of the Central Committee of the CPSU and its Presidium shall be renewed. Presidium members may, as a rule, be elected for not more than three successive terms. Particular Party workers, by virtue of their generally-recognized authority and high political, organizational and other abilities, may be elected successively to the leading bodies for a longer period. In that case, the respective candidate is considered elected, provided not less than three-quarters of the votes are cast for him by secret ballot.

Members of the Central Committees of the Communist parties of Union republics, of territorial and regional committees shall be renewed by not less than one-third at each regular election, and those of area, city and district committees, and the committees and bureaus of primary Party organizations shall be renewed by one-half. Furthermore, members of these leading Party bodies may be elected consecutively for not more than three terms, and secretaries of the primary Party organizations for not more than two consecutive terms.

In consideration of the political and professional qualities of a person, a Party organization may elect him to its leading body for a longer period. In that case a candidate is considered elected if not less than three-quarters of the Communists attending vote for him.

Party members not reelected to a leading Party body on the expiration of their terms may be reelected at subsequent elections.

A decision on the removal of a member from the CC of the CPSU and other leading organs shall be adopted solely by secret ballot, and is valid when not less than two-thirds of the members of the body concerned vote in favor of the decision.

(b) To extend the application of the elective principle and that of accountability in Party organizations at all levels, including Party organizations working under special conditions (Army, Navy).

(c) To enhance the role of Party meetings, conferences, congresses and plenary meetings of Party committees and other collective bodies. To provide favorable conditions for a free and business-like discussion within the Party of questions concerning its policy and practical activities, for comradely discussions of controversial or insufficiently clear matters.

(d) To reduce steadily the salaried Party staffs, enlisting Communists more extensively as non-salaried workers doing voluntary work.

(e) To develop criticism and self-criticism to the utmost as a tried and tested method of work and a means of disclosing and rectifying errors and shortcomings and properly educating cadres.

In the period of full-scale communist construction the role and responsibility of every Party member steadily will increase. It is the duty of a Communist, in production, in social and personal life, to be a model in the struggle for the development and consolidation of communist relations, and to observe the principles and norms of communist morality. The CPSU will reinforce its ranks with the most politically conscious and active working people, and keep pure and hold high the name of Communist.

The development of inner-Party democracy must ensure greater activity among Communists and enhance their responsibility for the realization of the noble ideals of communism. It will promote the cultivation in them of an inner, organic need to act always and in all matters in full accordance with the principles of the Party and its lofty aims.

The Party will continue to strengthen the unity and solidarity of its ranks, and to maintain the purity of Marxism-Leninism. The Party preserves such organizational guarantees as are provided by the Rules of the CPSU against all manifestations of factionalism and group activity incompatible with Marxist-Leninist party principles. *The unshakable ideological and organizational unity of the Party is the most important source of its invincibility, a guarantee for the successful solution of the great tasks of communist construction.*

The people are the decisive force in the building of communism. *The Party exists for the people, and it is in serving the people that it sees the purpose of its activity.* To further extend and deepen the ties between the Party and the people is an imperative condition of success in the struggle for communism. The Party considers it its duty always to consult the working people on the major questions of home and foreign policy, to make these questions an object of nation-wide discussion, and to attract the more extensive participation of non-members in all its work. The more socialist democracy develops, the broader and more versatile the work of the Party among the working people must be, and the stronger will be its influence among the masses.

The Party will in every way promote the extension and improvement of the work of the Soviets, the trade unions, the YCL, and other mass organizations of working people, and the development of the creative energy and initiative of the masses, and will strengthen the unity and friendship of all the peoples of the USSR.

The CPSU is an integral part of the international Communist and working-class movement. The tried and tested Marxist-Leninist principles of proletarian internationalism will continue to be inviolable principles which the Party will follow undeviatingly.

The Communist Party of the Soviet Union will continue to strengthen the unity of the international Communist movement, to develop fraternal ties with all the Communist and Workers' parties and to coordinate its actions with the efforts of all the contingents of the world Communist movement in the joint struggle against the danger of a new world war, for the interests of the working people, for peace, democracy, and socialism.

Such is the program of work for communist construction which the Communist Party of the Soviet Union has mapped out.

The achievement of communism in the USSR will be the greatest victory mankind has ever won throughout its long history. Every new step made towards the bright peaks of communism inspires the working masses in all countries, renders immense moral support to the struggle for the liberation of all peoples from social and national oppression, and brings closer the triumph of Marxism-Leninism on a world-wide scale.

When the Soviet people will enjoy the blessings of communism, new hundreds of millions of people on earth will say: "We are for communism!" It is not through war with other countries, but by the example of a more perfect organization of society, by rapid progress in developing the productive forces, the creation of all conditions for the happiness and well-being of man, that the ideas of communism win the minds and hearts of the masses.

The forces of social progress will inevitably grow in all countries, and this will assist the builders of communism in the Soviet Union.

The Party proceeds from Marxist-Leninist proposition: history is made by the people, and communism is a creation of the people, of its energy and intelligence. The victory of communism depends on people, and communism is built for people. Every Soviet man brings the triumph of communism nearer by his labor. The successes of communist construction spell abundance and a happy life to all, and enhance the might, prestige and glory of the Soviet Union.

The Party is confident that the Soviet people will accept the new Program of the CPSU as their own vital cause, as the greatest purpose of their life and as a banner of nation-wide struggle for the building of communism. The Party calls on all Communists, of the entire Soviet people—all working men and women, collective farmers and workers by brain—to apply their energies to the successful fulfilment of the historic tasks set forth in this Program.

Under the tried and tested leadership of the Communist Party, under the banner of Marxism-Leninism, the Soviet people have built socialism.

Under the leadership of the Party, under the banner of Marxism-Leninism, the Soviet people will build communist society.

The Party solemnly proclaims: the present generation of Soviet people shall live in communism!

27

DATE